Integrating Spirituality in Counseling: A Manual for Using the Experiential Focusing Method

Elfie Hinterkopf

AMERICAN
COUNSELING
ASSOCIATION

INTEGRATING SPIRITUALITY IN COUNSELING

10 9 8 7 6 5 4 3 2

American Counseling Association
5999 Stevenson Avenue
Alexandria, VA 22304

Director of Aquisitions
Carolyn Baker

Director of Publishing Systems
Michael Comlish

Library of Congress Cataloging-in Publication Data

Hinterkopf, Elfie.
    Integrating spirituality in counseling in a manual for using the experiential focusing method / Elfie Hinterkopf.
       p. cm.
    Includes bibliographical references and index.
    ISBN 1-55620-169-9 (alk. paper)
    1. Counseling 2. Psychotherapy. 3. Spiritual life. I. Title.
BF637.DS.H53   1998
156'.3—dc21
                                                  97-25828
                                                     CIP

Table of Contents

Foreword

*I*n the fall of 1995, I was privileged to be among 12 counseling professionals, mostly counselor educators, invited to Charlotte, North Carolina, for a Summit on Spirituality. The Summit was endorsed by the Association for Spiritual, Ethical and Religious Values in Counseling, a division of the American Counseling Association. Summit participants developed a description of spirituality; identified professional counselor competencies regarding religious, spiritual, and transpersonal dimensions of counseling; and outlined strategies for infusing spiritual aspects of counseling into counselor education programs. This pioneering endeavor reflects the consciousness of our times. It is in the context of this consciousness that Dr. Hinterkopf's book, *Integrating Spirituality in Counseling,* is such a timely contribution to the professional literature of counseling.

Synchronistically, it was also in the fall of 1995 that I invited Dr. Hinterkopf to the University of North Texas to conduct a training workshop for counselors and counselor trainees interested in the technique of Focusing as a way to integrate spirituality into counseling. The ramifications of this workshop have been far-reaching. A subgroup of the original attendees formed a biweekly practice group that continues to meet now, 4 months after the original workshop. Several of these opted to drive the 8 hours round trip between Dallas and Austin once a month for 3 months to receive advanced supervision from Dr. Hinterkopf. One of the original workshop attendees organized a second training workshop in Dallas and has additional workshops scheduled over the next few months.

These efforts speak to the attraction these counselors have felt to the power of the Experiential Focusing Method to address the spiritual dimension in counseling. In my 8 years as a counselor educator, I've rarely seen counselors respond with such enthusiasm to a specific technique or method. The counselors have commented repeatedly on how the Focusing Method enables appropriately oriented clients to move quickly into deep, "crux" aspects of their concerns. The counselors have remarked that new, surprising, and deeply healing material emerges routinely from Focusing. And they have expressed how much they value the counselor's role as a guide who facilitates the client's active participation and responsibility for what is generated throughout the process.

Dr. Hinterkopf's form of Focusing is a gentle yet direct method for addressing the spiritual aspects of any concern. Perhaps the most innovative feature of her approach is its attention to both spiritual content, which has received the lion's share of attention in the counseling literature to date, and spiritual process. Spiritual content refers to symbolized material with meanings idiosyncratic to each client, such as God, Allah, Mother Earth, and past life. Counselors are admonished to treat such content nonjudgmentally, an imperative for practice in the multicultural world in which we live. But what if the content seems to be destructive to the client? How can the counselor remain nonjudgmental yet guide the client in some form of evaluation of the content?

Herein lies the value of spiritual process which, according to Dr. Hinterkopf, involves paying attention to concrete, bodily feeling in a special way that allows the unfolding of greater easing and life energy. As each new aspect of content emerges, the counselor guides the client back to his or her body to notice any change in wholistic bodily sensation, referred to as "felt sense."

The client's experience of increased easing and life energy becomes the litmus test of "judging" the value of any particular spiritual content; except for a valuing of easing and life energy, the counselor is freed from judgment from any other source. I know of no other method that meets these criteria and, in addition, that involves the clear guidelines for practice that Dr. Hinterkopf provides in this book.

Within the context described above, it is easy to see how counselors can use the Experiential Focusing Method with religious as well as nonreligious clients. Counselors can help clients work through blocks to experiencing their spirituality, deepen existing spiritual experiences, or find new life-giving connections to the spiritual dimension. Using the Focusing Method, counselors can address client issues that fall under the *Diagnostic and Statistical Manual of Mental Disorders*, 4th edition category of Religious or Spiritual Problem. For example, it can be used to help clients evaluate distressing aspects of their religious background and deepen enhancing aspects. For the client in spiritual emergency, overwhelmed with the emergence of new spiritual material such as psychic or mystical experience, the Focusing Method provides strategies both for grounding and for working through the emergent material.

The Experiential Focusing Method can be used with any psychotherapeutic theory or model, including cognitive-behavioral, object relations, Gestalt, or client-centered. This eclectic appeal reflects the diversity of Dr. Hinterkopf's own background and spiritual search. The influences of her religious background, her study with Victor Frankl, her time in India, her study of anthropology, and her work with the originator of Focusing, Eugene Gendlin, are seen in this book.

Perhaps the strongest endorsement I can give is that I have found Focusing to be valuable in my own spiritual work. Whether addressing issues of which I'm consciously aware or the enigmatic aspects of dreams, I have discovered new nuances of spiritual meaning and found new healing, even forward movement, through this method.

Although Dr. Hinterkopf's writing is straightforward and clear, my experience is that her approach is best integrated into a counselor's repertoire through a process that is both didactic and experiential. It is through the experience and supervised practice of her technique that its subtlety and power can best be ascertained and accessed. The counselor who, in reading this book, feels an affinity for the process is encouraged to seek training through Focusing workshops and supervised practice.

In my experiences with Dr. Hinterkopf, it has become evident that she not only teaches Focusing, but she also lives it. For her, Focusing is not just a technique but a way of being that shines through her presence. Like the Focusing method, she exudes a simple elegance without superfluous complexity. She works gently, yet powerfully, to help people transform their lives. This book is written with the clarity needed to help other mental health professionals do some of the same kind of work.

Janice Holden
Denton, Texas

Preface

This book presents a groundbreaking method, called Focusing, to enable mental health professionals to integrate the spiritual dimension in their counseling. The Experiential Focusing Method may be used to help clients work through religious and spiritual problems, deepen existing spiritual experiences, and facilitate new, life-giving connections to spirituality.

Chapter 1, Spiritual Wellness and Focusing, discusses the need for this book, presents a spiritual wellness model, and shows how the Focusing Method can be used to facilitate spiritual development in clients. Other benefits of using the Focusing Method in counseling are described.

Chapter 2, Defining the Spiritual Experience, presents a process definition of spirituality that includes the spiritual experiences of all clients in counseling and psychotherapy. The distinction between process and content brings clarity to the subject of spirituality in counseling. An example of using Focusing to help a client experience his or her spirituality is given, and implications for practice are discussed.

Chapter 3, Integrating Spirituality Through Focusing, presents a brief history of the research that led to the development of the Focusing Method. Two key terms in Focusing, *felt sense* and *felt shift*, are explained and related to spirituality. Examples are provided, and implications for practice are considered.

Chapter 4, Focusing Attitudes, explains attitudes that are needed toward oneself and one's process when Focusing. These attitudes include being receptive, expectant, accepting, patient, friendly, and kind. The author offers suggestions for helping clients learn these attitudes, illustrated with examples from counseling sessions.

Chapter 5, Keeping a Certain Distance, provides instructions, illustrated with examples, to help clients keep a certain distance toward problems. Finding a certain distance is related to the spiritual wellness model. Finding a certain distance may be used to help both clients in spiritual emergency and clients in spiritual repression return to a more centered position from which they can experience spiritual development.

Chapter 6, Focusing and the Inner Critic, presents guidelines to help clients distinguish "the still, small voice" of the Focusing process from the inner critic. Three approaches for working with the inner critic are presented: (a) distinguishing Focusing from the inner critic, (b) finding a stronger position than the critic, and (c) Focusing on a felt sense associated with the critic. The third way involves helping clients transform and integrate this aspect of themselves.

Chapter 7, Six Focusing Steps, describes steps that are used to teach clients Focusing. The author presents an example of leading a client through a six-step Focusing process that leads to spiritual growth. Practical suggestions to help counselors decide when to use Focusing to integrate spirituality in counseling are given, and various uses of the Focusing Method are described.

Chapter 8, Asking, presents powerful Focusing questions that facilitate the psychospiritual growth process in clients. Examples from counseling sessions and guidelines for using the questions to facilitate spiritual development are given.

Chapter 9, Working With Spiritual Process, offers guidelines for facilitating a client's psychospiritual process through Focusing. By learning to facilitate a client's process, a counselor can develop a more open attitude toward unfamiliar spiritual content. Examples in this chapter illustrate how to help clients work through a variety of spiritual issues, including those involving spiritual emergency and spiritual repression.

Chapter 10, Special Considerations Regarding Content, provides guidelines for working with spiritual content in counseling. Special considerations include learning about the client's religious tradition or spiritual orientation, using the client's terminology, and asking spiritually oriented Focusing questions to facilitate psychospiritual growth. Contraindications for using such questions are discussed.

Chapter 11, An Excerpt From a Psychotherapy Session, presents therapeutic responses that are examined to show how they help facilitate spiritual growth. The excerpt illustrates asking Focusing questions, giving Focusing suggestions, and guiding a client through several rounds of the Six Steps of Focusing.

Chapter 12, How Counselors Can Explore Their Own Spirituality, summarizes some of the professional counselor competencies regarding the spiritual dimension in counseling endorsed by the Association for Spiritual, Ethical and Religious Values in Counseling, a division of the American Counseling Association. Training to meet these competencies involves helping counselors explore their own spirituality. For this purpose a workshop description and Focusing exercises are included in the chapter.

In Appendix A, the author presents a set of Focusing instructions in a format for one person to read to another. Counselors can use these instructions to practice Focusing with each other before applying the method in a therapeutic setting.

Resources for learning Focusing can be found in Appendix B.

About the Author

Elfie Hinterkopf, Ph.D. is an international workshop leader and licensed professional counselor in private practice in Austin, Texas. She has an M.A. in anthropology and a Ph.D. in counseling psychology. She studied the Experiential Focusing Method with its originator, Dr. Eugene Gendlin, at the University of Chicago, has been teaching Focusing for more than 20 years, and has published numerous journal articles on Focusing. Dr. Hinterkopf taught counseling psychology at the graduate level for many years, directed a National Institute of Mental Health research project, and served as a Peace Corps volunteer in India. She has been a national presenter for the American Counseling Association and has received a grant from the Association for Spiritual, Ethical and Religious Values in Counseling to help her develop her ideas for this book.

Acknowledgments

*I*especially wish to thank my good friend Les Brunswick for his generous and invaluable editing and feedback and for some of his concepts that are included in this book. My thanks also go to Peter Campbell and Ed McMahon for their feedback, for suggesting the term *caring, feeling presence* used in Chapter 12, and for publishing some of my earlier articles in *Kairos*. Ann Weiser Cornell published many of my articles in *The Focusing Connection*, and she and Jay Cornell edited a draft of this book. One of my earlier papers, "Focusing and Spirituality in Counseling," was published in *The Folio: A Journal for Focusing and Experiential Therapy*. The feedback received from readers of this article helped me broaden my definition of the spiritual experience. M. Harry Daniels, editor, gave helpful suggestions for revising my article, "Integrating Spiritual Experiences in Counseling: The Use of Focusing," for publication in *Counseling and Values*.

I would like to thank the Association for Spiritual, Ethical and Religious Values in Counseling, a division of the American Counseling Association, for a grant to develop my ideas and evaluate my workshops on integrating spirituality in counseling. John Shea's book, *Religious Experiencing: William James and Eugene Gendlin* (1987), inspired me to begin work on a definition of the spiritual experience. My discussions with Daniel Helminiak helped me develop a definition of spirituality that embraces the spirituality of all human beings.

My thanks go to Donna Frysinger, Bala Jaison, Julie Kirby, Michael Kirkpatrick, Lianne Mercer, and Judy Shetler for their helpful comments and editing and to Luke Lukens and Ann Marie Wallace for their useful feedback.

I am grateful to my brother Peter Hinterkopf and his wife Mimi for showing me that their conservative religious experiences have deep meaning in their lives. I am also grateful to my father, who had the good sense to make the rule in our home that all (five) religions would be tolerated. Partly, this book was written to reconcile the conflicting religious views in my family of origin. My work with Focusing and spirituality helped me reconcile these seemingly conflicting views within myself.

I especially want to express my gratitude to Eugene Gendlin for his feedback and for teaching me to listen to the still, small voice inside. His teaching helped me learn to trust my own inner process. At times I had difficulty learning Focusing, but he gave me encouragement by saying that the people who have the most difficulty learning Focusing often become the best teachers. I would like to thank him for showing me how a professor can encourage and elevate his students, thereby helping them do even better than they had imagined.

In this book I will frequently use the word *counselor* to refer to all types of mental health professionals, including professional counselors, pastoral counselors, drug and alcohol abuse counselors, social workers, psychiatric nurses, psychologists, psychiatrists, and others in the helping professions. I use the terms *counselor* and *counseling* because I hope that these terms will be the most inclusive in their meaning. This book was also written for spiritual directors, religious educators, peer counselors, and anyone wishing to be a helpful companion.

My Search for Meaning

We all search for meaning in our lives. Some of us look for it in our work, some of us look for it in relationships, some of us look for it in counseling, and some of us even look for it in other cultures. My search for meaning brought me to Focusing and spirituality.

I was brought up in a legalistic, Christian, fundamentalist home. At the age of 13 I had to choose between joining the church and dancing. I chose dancing. Christianity with all its "shoulds" and "shouldn'ts" and separatism seemed meaningless to me. Several years later, when I rejected the religion that had permeated my life, I felt a sense of meaninglessness. So I started what I called my search for meaning.

I took my first major step while I was attending college. I decided to go to the University of Vienna in Austria to study with Victor Frankl, who had written *Man's Search for Meaning* (1984). Frankl was a Jewish psychiatrist who had survived European concentration camps. He noticed that some people in the camps had the will to live, whereas others gave up and died. He observed that this was not a matter of physical strength or make-up. People who had the will to live had at least one of three things in their lives: (a) faith in God, (b) creative work, or (c) someone to love. However, when I asked Victor Frankl, he couldn't tell me how to find meaning because I didn't have any of these three things. Once he said that meaning was found inside, but this made no sense to me at that time in my life. I did not know what to do to find meaning inside. I left Vienna feeling frustrated about my search.

My next step was to try to find meaning by helping other people. I joined the Peace Corps and went to India. There I found interesting work, but it did not give me the meaning I was looking for. I chose India because I hoped to find meaning in the practice of Indian meditation. In India I found a guru with whom I studied. During meditation I experienced becoming peaceful, but afterward I still had the same confused feelings and painful problems in my life, mostly stemming from childhood. As I left India, I felt discouraged about my search for meaning.

Then I decided to try to find meaning by discovering it in the right culture, so I began graduate studies in anthropology. I studied what individuals and groups of people did, but this did not help *me* find meaning in *my* life. As part of my studies, I did field work with the Apaches on an Indian reservation in Arizona. A large percentage of the people were alcoholics. I found it difficult to communicate with them and felt isolated and lonely. I went from feeling discouraged to feeling hopeless about my search for meaning.

When I returned to Chicago to study for my doctoral exams, I met Dr. Eugene Gendlin, a psychologist and philosopher at the University of Chicago. Gendlin talked about finding meaning by listening to the "still, small voice inside," or by listening to one's inner process in a special way. He not only talked about finding meaning, as Victor Frankl had, but he taught me specific steps for what I needed to do inside to discover a sense of meaningfulness. He called this method *Focusing* (Gendlin, 1981). Gendlin saw Focusing as a deeply creative process through which people could experience meaning as they worked through personal problems in psychotherapy. For the first time I felt hopeful about finding an answer to my search for meaning.

Focusing has helped me find meaning and purpose in my life in at least three ways. First, I frequently experienced meaning in my Focusing process as my inner process unfolded, as that which was unclear became more clear and usually symbolized. This same process is found at the core of creativity. Learning to become aware of my creative process gave me a sense of meaning.

Second, as I experienced easing, relief, and more life energy, and learned to value these experiences as guides for living, I began to sense direction, meaning, and purpose in my life. I became more clear about how I wished to lead my life. I became more aware of my likes and dislikes, for example, the kinds of people I wanted to associate with, how I wanted to spend leisure time, and the preferred nature of my work.

Third, as I practiced Focusing over time, like many others, I became more aware of my inner connection to the transcendent dimension. During my healing process, I began to experience myself in a larger context, as part of a larger whole. I began to experience my connectedness to more parts of myself, to others, and to life. I also began to experience God as a living reality. My faith was no longer based only on mental concepts. I learned that my inner process could be explored endlessly, and I became familiar with the mystery, wonder, and awe that came from this exploration.

The relationship between the Focusing process and spirituality can be difficult to describe logically. This relationship was expressed nicely with an image told to me by a client: "Focusing is like going down into a deep well. I start down the well by going through the problems and differences that isolate me. But the deeper I go, the more I feel at one with God, with humanity, and with all creation."

Because this process helped me in my own life, I changed fields of study, from anthropology to counseling psychology, to become a psychotherapist. I wanted to help others work through their problems and find a sense of meaning.

Thus far I have shared my own search. Each person has his or her own unique journey. Focusing can help each person find the next step on that journey.

For over 20 years, I have used and further developed the Experiential Focusing Method to help clients integrate spiritual experiences in counseling. I have observed that use of Focusing has great power in facilitating both religious and nonreligious spiritual experiences in my clients. While using Focusing I repeatedly observed that clients who initially felt heavy, constricted, dull, and stuck had those feelings transformed into expanded, transcending, and life-giving experiences.

This book has grown out of the joy and excitement that I experienced while observing thousands of my clients and students using Focusing. It also grew out of my own experiences while practicing Focusing for 25 years.

Gendlin (1996) has said that the most important thing in therapy, the essence of working with another person, is to be present as a living being to the person in front of you. You, the therapist, need to wait for that person, that being in there, to be in contact with you. In other words, the therapeutic relationship is primary. Any method, including the Focusing Method, is secondary to this relationship.

The goal of counseling is the development of the whole person: mind, body, and spirit integrated together. Focusing is the sine qua non of wholistic therapy. It is not just body plus mind plus spirit put together. The Focusing Method helps us access that which is whole in us *before* it is split apart. As Campbell (1996) has so eloquently said, with Focusing "we touch into the unpredictability of human spirit manifesting itself within the body's forward movement into some Greater Wholeness." I hope that this book, which describes my way of teaching the Focusing Method, will serve as a door to help you and your clients experience that Greater Wholeness.

Spiritual Wellness and Focusing

The Need for This Book

Spirituality is part of the basic human experience, and spiritual issues arise frequently in counseling. For example, a client might say, "My relationship with Jesus Christ is important to me," "I have negative feelings about God," "I've been religious all my life, but I've never had an experience of God," or "Experiences from my past lives are overwhelming me." Counselors need to be able to respond sensitively to any one of these situations to facilitate a process that leads to spiritual growth. Furthermore, counselors need to be able to facilitate spiritual growth even when the client's beliefs differ from their own.

Although spirituality is an important part of counseling, mental health professionals rarely receive training to work with these issues. Increasingly, counselors are asking for information about how to integrate the spiritual dimension into their practice. A further problem exists in that counselors are faced with clients from many different cultures with a wide range of spiritual problems. Many counselors are asking for experiential approaches to spirituality that are multicultural and nonjudgmental.

This book presents a breakthrough method called Focusing that enables mental health professionals to integrate the spiritual dimension in their counseling. Focusing was originally developed by Dr. Eugene Gendlin, an existential-phenomenological psychologist and philosopher at the University of Chicago, to help clients be more successful in psychotherapy (Gendlin,1969,1981). The method is a powerful tool to identify, describe, and facilitate the spiritual growth process during psychotherapy.

The Focusing approach may be used with all clients, whether they follow a particular religion or none at all. Because the method can be used with any religious or spiritual experience, it is especially appropriate for use in multicultural contexts. Even a counselor who has a nonreligious orientation can use the Focusing Method to help clients explore their religious and spiritual experiences.

Focusing offers a tool to help clients experience and develop spirituality while working through issues traditionally considered to be psychotherapeutic. Because Focusing involves paying attention to whatever is presently felt in the body, it is almost impossible to avoid or deny psychotherapeutic issues. Thus, use of the Focusing Method avoids a disadvantage found in some religious and spiritual approaches that may bypass psychological issues.

Counselors may sometimes feel confused about which parts of a client's religious experiences are abusive and which parts are life-affirming. Focusing offers a way for both counselors and clients to discern these differences. This is done by checking the client's felt religious experience to see if it brings easing and more life energy.

This same guideline may be applied to the use of any psychotherapeutic method. Thus, the Focusing Method may be incorporated into whatever psychotherapeutic approach a therapist is already using to make it more effective (Gendlin, 1996). Counselors need not change their style or principles to make use of Focusing.

In the remainder of this chapter I present a spiritual wellness model that clarifies some of the challenges counselors face when working with the spiritual issues of their clients. Ways in which the Focusing method can meet these challenges are discussed, and more specific benefits that result from using the method in counseling are described.

A Spiritual Wellness Model

The Focusing Method may be used in counseling for the remediation of religious and spiritual problems, the enhancement of already existing spiritual experiences, and the facilitation of new, life-giving connections to spirituality. All three of these processes are essential for spiritual wellness.

Chandler, Holden, and Kolander (1992) have presented a model for spiritual wellness (see Figure 1.1) that I have adapted to describe how the Focusing Method may be used with spiritual problems.

The model is based on the concept of spiritual development. According to Chandler et al. (1992), spiritual development is the process of incorporating spiritual experience that results ultimately in spiritual transformation.

People may be in one of two states that block spiritual development and need remediation: spiritual emergency or spiritual

Figure 1.1 Spiritual Wellness Model

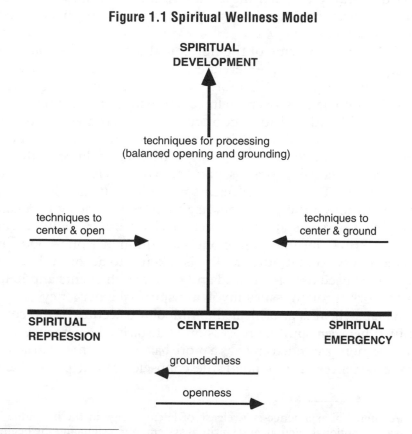

repression. In either case, the counselor helps by facilitating the client's movement to a more centered state in which the client's spiritual development may progress.

At one extreme on the horizontal dimension in Figure 1.1 is spiritual repression. Spiritual repression means that one denies or defies the spiritual tendency within oneself to defend against the pain of disillusionment (Chandler et al., 1992). The person at this end of the continuum might be out of touch with the spiritual dimension or have a block to spiritual experiences. Many clients (and counselors) have difficulty finding their own spirituality because of negative childhood experiences associated with religious practices. Focusing may be used to work through such blocks to help clients be more open to the spiritual dimension. In the process of working through these blocks, the client may integrate positive aspects of past religious experiences, resulting in increased spiritual wellness.

At the other extreme of the horizontal dimension is spiritual emergency. In spiritual emergency, spiritual material comes in an amount too great or in a form too foreign to be readily integrated. The client is overwhelmed by distressing feelings and preoccupied with spiritual content, to the detriment of other dimensions of wellness such as vocational, relational, or personal. For example, the client might be overwhelmed with visions, near-death experiences, past life experiences, or Kundalini experiences.[1] These clients need "grounding" (Chandler et al., 1992). Although these authors use the term *grounding* to mean bringing a person's attention exclusively to outer reality, I will use the term to mean bringing one's attention into one's body in a special way so that outer reality is taken into account. Focusing can be used to help ground and center such clients and help them work through issues involving spiritual emergency.

When a client is at or near the midpoint or center of the continuum between spiritual repression and spiritual emergency, the client is more grounded and has a more balanced openness to spiritual experiences. At this point, the counselor can help the client

---

[1]A Kundalini experience is a release of latent energy in the individual's physical, emotional, mental, and spiritual system, often signaling the beginning of a spiritual awakening. The energy may range from subtle to overwhelming. Kundalini experiences can be accompanied by a variety of symptoms, including extreme heat, visions, and sounds.

move along the vertical dimension of spiritual development. The counselor can use Focusing to do this by helping the client deepen and develop spiritual experiences that already exist as well as by helping the client have new, life-enhancing, spiritual experiences.

Specific Benefits

In addition to facilitating spiritual development in clients, the Experiential Focusing Method frequently results in a number of more specific benefits (Hinterkopf, 1988). Some of these benefits include learning the following:

1. **Be still and listen within.** When clients practice Focusing, they learn to be quiet and listen to the still, small voice within. Learning to listen to the inner voice, or the real self, helps clients access their creative source and their inner wisdom. Thus Focusing is self-empowering. In the Judeo-Christian tradition this is sometimes known as listening to God or the Holy Spirit. Some Buddhist clients report that Focusing helps them reach a state of emptiness and stillness.
2. **Adopt receptive, accepting, friendly, and patient attitudes.** Adopting a receptive attitude in Focusing helps clients learn to approach experiences with more relaxed attention that can loosen habitual ways of experiencing the self. This skill is needed for meditative mindfulness found in Buddhism. Learning to adopt accepting, friendly, and patient attitudes toward their feelings helps clients experience love, including God's love.
3. **Give up trying to control that which cannot be controlled.** Realizing that they do not control the content of what comes in Focusing helps clients learn to give up trying to control that which they cannot control. This is an attitude that most spiritual disciplines teach. Many theistic clients (those believing in a god or gods) have reported that learning to clear a space helps them experience "how it *really* feels to give things to God." For example, some monotheists have said that they previously gave things to God mentally, but now they are able to give things to God with their whole beings, including body, mind, and spirit.
4. **Distinguish the "still, small voice" from the "inner critic."** Many clients are confused when they begin inner exploration because they do not know how to distinguish between the still,

small voice and the inner critic. Focusing brings clarity. Clients are taught that what comes from Focusing brings easing and more life energy; what comes from the inner critic brings more tension and dullness. Of course, it is important to teach clients not to dissociate themselves from the inner critic but to Focus on that part of themselves to transform and integrate it. Some theistic clients report that this helps them distinguish that which comes from God and the Holy Spirit from that which comes from the inner critic. The Focusing Method helps clients discover and trust their real selves.

5. **Ask the most effective questions.** Many questions that clients ask in counseling lead to dead ends. Learning the "Asking" step in Focusing teaches clients to ask powerful, open-ended "what" questions (rather than "why" questions or closed-ended questions) to explore their inner process and receive new information. For example, clients are taught to ask, "What's the worst of this for me?" or "What does this whole thing need?" rather than "Why did this happen to me?" Clients within the theistic tradition frequently report that this in turn helps them learn to ask the best questions of God and the Holy Spirit.

6. **Develop a mindful, observer self or witness.** Many clients in counseling are overwhelmed by painful feelings. In Focusing clients learn to develop a mindful, observer self by keeping the right distance from their problems (i.e., far enough away to realize that their lives are greater than their problems but close enough to be aware of how they feel about various problems). In Buddhism this observer self or mindful self is sometimes referred to as a witness. Some theistic clients report that keeping the right distance helps them experience God as greater than their problems without denying the reality of their problems.

7. **Experience forgiveness.** Finding the right distance and seeing the "whole thing" often helps clients understand and accept parts of themselves that they previously considered unacceptable. Realizing that they are continually in the process of changing helps clients to be less judgmental of themselves and others. Theistic clients have reported that these aspects of Focusing have helped them experience God's forgiveness.

8. **Develop faith that their next healing step will come.** Many clients in psychotherapy have lost hope that their lives will improve. Learning to trust that their next healing step will come

in the Focusing process helps clients develop an attitude of faith. Some clients report that learning this attitude of faith has helped them unlock the spiritual growth process.

9. **Have a sense of meaning and purpose in life.** Clients who are burdened with problems almost always lack a sense of meaning and purpose in their lives. Focusing helps clients have meaning and purpose in their lives in several ways. Meaning and creativity are frequently experienced as the felt sense unfolds, that is, as that which is unclear becomes more clear (usually symbolized). As clients become more aware of experiences of easing and life-giving energy and learn to value these experiences as guides for living, they gain a sense of purpose and direction in their lives. In addition, during the healing process of Focusing over time, clients report that they are able to experience themselves in a larger context, as connected to a larger whole.

10. **Develop personal strength and autonomy.** As clients learn to trust their inner process, they learn to become more inner directed and less outer directed. In some cases, spiritual development may take the form of becoming more assertive and gaining more of a sense of themselves as individuals. In other cases, as clients become more aware of their connectedness to a larger background, to something greater than themselves, or to the divine, they become less afraid of being existentially alone. They may learn that their inner process can be explored endlessly, and they experience more of the mystery, wonder, and awe that come from exploring this process.

11. **Make religious faith more of an experiential reality.** Clients report that the use of Focusing helps them experience their faith and allows this experience to deepen and grow. Because Focusing is bodily based, this experiential knowledge goes beyond having only intellectual concepts about their faith. Theistic clients frequently report that this helps them experience God at a deeper level or with their whole being.

Conclusion

This chapter describes the power of using the Focusing Method to meet the spiritual needs of clients in counseling. Counselors may use Focusing to help open clients in spiritual repression and ground clients in spiritual emergency. When clients are open to spiritual development, the method may be used to deepen and facilitate spiritual experiences. Numerous benefits for facilitating spirituality in counseling result from using the method.

Defining the Spiritual Experience

A clear definition of spirituality can enable counselors to respond more sensitively to their clients. Although much thought has been given to the topic of spirituality, confusion still exists as to how it should be defined for purposes of counseling.

Two confusions that need to be resolved to arrive at a clear definition of spirituality are the difference between spirituality and religiousness and the question of theism and nontheism. These issues can be resolved through Gendlin's theory of experiencing (1961, 1964).

The first issue relates to the difference between spirituality and religiousness. In this book the term *religiousness* is used to mean adherence to the beliefs and practices of an organized church or religious institution (Shafranske & Malony, 1990). *Spirituality* is used to refer to a unique, personally meaningful experience (Shafranske & Gorsuch, 1984). Although spirituality may include various forms of religiousness, spirituality does not necessarily involve religiousness. A clear definition of spirituality helps counselors respond to their clients' spiritual issues whether a client's spirituality is associated with a religion or not.

The second issue relates to theism and nontheism. Most talk about spirituality in Western tradition makes reference to something greater than ourselves, such as God, a Higher Power, or the divine. On the other hand, psychotherapists who have divorced themselves from religious organizations sometimes borrow from Eastern traditions and talk about spirituality in terms of "extraordinary" events, such as visions and, near-death-like, past life, and out-of-body experiences. At times they omit mention of God or the divine. Because many people are spiritual but not theistic, a comprehensive definition of spirituality for use in counseling separates spirituality from religious reference to God or the divine. At the same time a comprehensive definition of spirituality includes the rich expression of religious reference to God or the divine frequently associated with spirituality.

In dealing with spiritual issues, the counselor needs to respond sensitively so that a growth-producing process can occur for the client. However, if the counselor has a definition of spirituality that excludes some type of content—for example, spirituality is only that which is connected to an organized religion or theism or extraordinary events—then the counselor might respond insensitively to content that does not fit that definition.

The purpose of this chapter is to present a definition of spirituality that is not restricted by the nature of spiritual content but instead includes the spirituality of all clients by concentrating on spiritual process. A case example of using the Experiential Focusing Method to facilitate spiritual process is presented, and implications of a process definition of spirituality for the practice of counseling are discussed.

Need for a Process Definition of Spirituality

I have found that Gendlin's theory of experiencing (1961, 1964) brings clarity to the confusion found in defining spirituality. Gendlin has made an important distinction between *process* and *content* in psychotherapy. He has described the experiencing *process* as paying attention to vague, implicit, bodily feelings in a special way so that they unfold and bring new explicit meanings that result in physiological relief or release. He has said that *content* involves symbolizations, or what the process is about. Applying this distinction to spirituality, content might involve words such as God, Christ, Mother Earth, Allah, Higher Power, and past-life, near-death, and extrasensory perception (ESP) material.

The distinction between process and content is crucial in the practice of counseling in general and for integrating spirituality in counseling in particular. The counselor needs to be able to follow process in therapy to determine whether a response or an intervention has been helpful to a client, that is, has an intervention made a felt difference in a client or merely a mental difference? Content words, such as *God*, have different connotations or meanings for each individual. If a counselor concentrates on spiritual content to the exclusion of process, especially when encountering unfamiliar spiritual content, the counselor may risk becoming judgmental.

My goal in defining spirituality was to develop a definition that would be useful in psychotherapy and counseling and would include the spiritual experiences of all clients in counseling (Hinterkopf, 1994, 1995b). This definition would point to the client's experience of spirituality, which would be beneficial to the client's growth.

Therefore I am proposing the following definition of spirituality or the spiritual experience: *a subtle, bodily feeling with vague meanings that brings new, clearer meanings involving a transcendent growth process.*

First, the spiritual experience involves *a subtle, bodily feeling with vague meanings.* The client has a vague, subtle feeling that can be attended to in the body at the present time. Spirituality involves subtle feelings, a bodily sense, and not simply a cognitive belief system. For example, a client may have a vaguely good feeling that involves a large sense of peace and calm in the chest or a vaguely uncomfortable feeling that includes a sense of emptiness in the torso area. The feelings are subtle, elusive, hard to describe, and more than can be put into words. The feelings are not just single emotions such as happy or afraid. They can be located in the body, for example in the throat, chest, or stomach. The vague, complex feelings carry implicitly felt meanings or meanings that are only vaguely felt. The exact meaning is not yet known.

Second, this subtle, bodily feeling with vague meanings *brings new, clearer meanings.* "Bring" implies that people frequently perceive that they do not cause these new, explicit meanings to occur. At first the client senses an unclear feeling that carries only implicit meanings. As the client continues to pay attention to the unclear, subtle feeling in a gentle, caring way, new meanings unfold and become more clear. For example, as a client pays attention to a vague feeling of peace and calm, the client may receive a new, explicit meaning or understanding of accepting another person's differences.

Third, a spiritual experience *involves a transcendent growth process.* "Transcend" means to move beyond one's former frame of reference in a direction of higher or broader scope, a more inclusive perspective. Such transcendence is essential to human growth. A transcendent growth process, found in all human beings, involves moving beyond one's own unhealthy egocentricity, duality, and exclusivity toward more healthy egocentricity, inclusivity, unity, and a capacity to love (Chandler et al., 1992). The movement from unhealthy to healthy egocentricity might involve the ability to become more assertive or the increased ability to stand one's ground.

Gendlin (1996) has described this growth process in the following way:

> When a person's central core or inward self expands it strengthens and develops, the "I" becomes stronger. The person—I mean that which looks out from behind the eyes—comes more into its own.
>
> One develops when the desire to live and do things stirs deep down, when one's own hopes and desires stir, when one's own perceptions and evaluations carry a new sureness, when the capacity to stand one's ground increases, and when one can consider others and their needs. One comes to feel one's separate existence solidly enough to want to be close to others as they really are. It is development when one is drawn to something that is directly interesting, and when one wants to play. It is development when something stirs inside that has long been immobile and silent, cramped and almost dumb, and when life's energy flows in a new way. (pp. 21–22)

Spiritual growth involves bodily felt release, more life energy, feeling more fully present and whole, a sense of feeling larger and being able to accept or reach out to more parts of oneself, to more people, and to more of life (Campbell & McMahon, 1985). For example, a client feeling peace and calm who receives a new understanding of "accepting another person's differences" may have the growth experience of accepting others more as they are, thus reaching out to more people. After a spiritual experience, growth usually occurs in many areas of the client's life.

When I taught Focusing in Japan, the importance of a process definition of spirituality for cross-cultural counseling was confirmed by participants in my workshops. In the West people often think of spirituality as involving more self-transcendence and love for others (content terms). The Japanese are raised with the assumption of oneness and unity with other people and their environment. Their language reflects this assumption. Personal pro-nouns, such as I and you, are frequently omitted from sentences. For the Japanese the process of spiritual growth tends to involve developing more healthy egocentricity, more of a sense of indi-viduality and separation. When Westerners speak of spirituality in terms of unity and self-transcendence (content terms), Japa-nese people may have the reaction that they don't need spiritual-ity. When I spoke about spirituality in process terms (implicit feelings unfolding into more explicit meanings that bring more easing and life energy), they could see the relevance of spirituality in their own lives.

This definition of spirituality includes what is often referred to as *transpersonal experiences.* Transpersonal experiences involve an expansion or extension of consciousness beyond the usual ego boundaries and beyond the limitations of time or space (Grof, 1976). Spiritual process may include transpersonal experiences, such as intuitive, psychic, and mystical experiences. Also, when referring to spiritual content, I assume that transpersonal content is included.

The growth involved in spiritual experiences is often essential for personal development. However, for various reasons, the client's experiencing may be "stuck," "structure-bound," or incomplete. When this is the case, the question for counselors is what can be done to help develop and facilitate the spiritual experience. At this point the Experiential Focusing Method may be applied.

The reason that the Focusing Method is useful in this type of problematic situation is that every spiritual experience has a subtle, bodily feeling with vague meanings. When a client Focuses on a subtle, bodily felt meaning, it usually results in spiritual growth. Therefore, when growth is not occurring, the Focusing Method may be used to promote it.

Example of Using Focusing to Help a Client Experience Her Spirituality

This example demonstrates how I used Focusing to help a client experience her spirituality in a way that involved more separa-tion from her father, as well as a sense of becoming more whole. I am sharing highlights of the session that illustrate the client's spiritual experience along with a few of my therapeutic responses.

The actual time taken for this part of the session was about 20 minutes.

> Mary, a seminary student, said that she wanted to work on the difficulty she had in finding a time to pray. She mentioned that "something seemed to be in the way" of her "taking time just to be with God." It didn't make sense because she now had more free time in her schedule than in previous semesters.
>
> I invited her to take time to pay attention inside to that "something" that seemed to be in the way. I said that she could describe the feeling to me when she had the words. (Words such as "something," "sort of," and "kind of like" frequently indicate unclear feelings with vague meanings. At such times it is helpful for the counselor to invite the client to take the time to sense into these vague feelings.)
>
> After about 45 seconds she said that she had "a vague nauseated feeling that felt like gagging along with fear and anxiety in her chest and stomach." She said that she was astonished to have such negative feelings about something that she really wanted to do. I suggested that she stay with the whole feeling in a gentle, caring way and notice what it had to tell her.
>
> After almost a minute she cried and said that it felt like being alone with her father who had sexually abused her. She realized that she had confused time alone with God with time alone with her father. She reported a feeling of release that corresponded with her realization. In the next session Mary reported that she had been able to have a daily prayer time.

This example involves a spiritual process, not because it involved God (spiritual content), but because it involved a vague bodily feeling with unclear meanings that, when gently attended to, brought new explicit meanings along with felt release. In Mary's case the transcendent growth process involved accepting more parts of herself as separate from her father, along with a sense of feeling more whole in her relationship with God.

A transcendent growth process may, but does not necessarily, involve a deity or higher power. Some clients refer to a deity or higher power by such names as *God, Christ, Allah, Mother Earth, Higher Power,* or *universal energy.* Other clients, not referring to a deity or higher power, may report that their spirituality is found in service to others, the environmental movement, or more assertiveness. A transcendent growth process may involve associated qualities, such as faith, love, interconnectedness, living in the flow (the Tao), allowing (rather than trying to control), and nonattachment (Lukens, 1992). A spiritual experience may also involve existential questions, such as questions of meaning and purpose, because such questions frequently lead a person's attention in a direction of higher or broader scope.

Implications for Practice

The use of such a broad process definition of spirituality can help a client integrate seemingly conflicting parts within himself or herself regarding spiritual issues. This definition can help the person rise to a broader view so that he or she can embrace aspects of both parts. For example, one client who had conflicting parts that she had introjected from her Christian mother and agnostic father was able to integrate the life-giving parts from both parents. In addition, she was able to reject aspects of both parts that were not life affirming. The result was a reduction of inner conflict and an increased sense of peace within herself.

Although the spiritual experience is usually a dramatic or life changing moment, it is almost always part of a larger growth process. Before the dramatic moment there are often many small steps or movements. For example, the client may make a new distinction or connection or give his or her perceptions more recognition than before. Such small steps may be seen as part of the spiritual growth process and need to be affirmed by the psychotherapist.

In counseling, the therapist needs to let the client decide whether a particular experience is spiritual. However, if a client asks a counselor whether an experience is spiritual, I believe it is important that a counselor give at least a brief definition of spirituality to explain his or her response. For example, if a client asks me whether I think his or her experience was spiritual, I might answer, "Yes, if I define spirituality as a special kind of experience in which one reaches out to more parts of oneself, others, and life."

My definition of the spiritual experience assumes that psychological growth and spiritual growth are synonymous (Helminiak, 1987). It must be remembered that this is a process definition, not a content definition. Although the *content* of a spiritual experience, such as God, Christ, or Higher Power, may be extremely inspiring because it carries such rich, implicit meanings for a particular person, my definition is concerned with the psychospiritual change *process*. To describe the psychospiritual change process in which many growth events occur, the term *psychospiritual experiencing* may be used.

For some purposes it is useful to make a distinction between spiritual and psychological content. However, for counseling, what is essential is that the same growth process is involved with both. This means that a counselor who is familiar with psychological issues need not turn away from the client when spiritual issues arise. Rather, the counselor can continue to use the same methods, including Focusing, to facilitate growth. Similarly, spiritual directors can also work with psychological issues when they arise. Of course, in either case, a referral should be made when issues arise that are beyond the helper's expertise.

Any definition of spirituality that depends solely on content will be judgmental because it will exclude some people. Judging whether a client's experience is spiritual or not, based on content or on the client's words, has the disadvantage that words such as *God, Allah,* or *Christ* have different meanings or connotations for each person. Instead, this decision can be based on the client's experiencing process. For example, does the client feel more easing and life energy? Is the client able to accept or reach out to more parts of himself or herself, to others, and to more of life?

Conclusion

This chapter has shown how Gendlin's theory of experiencing can be used to develop a definition of spirituality useful for the practice of counseling. The use of such a process definition has many advantages; most importantly, it can include the diverse spiritual experiences of all clients in counseling. In the next chapter I describe how Gendlin used his theory of experiencing to develop the Focusing Method. It will be seen that the client's attention to experiential process is vital both for spiritual growth and for success in psychotherapy.

CHAPTER

Integrating Spirituality Through Focusing

This chapter presents a brief history of the research that led to the development of the Focusing Method, and the Focusing Method is introduced. Two key Focusing terms, *felt sense* and *felt shift,* are explained and related to spirituality. Examples are provided, and implications for practice are considered.

A Brief History of Focusing

Eugene Gendlin began his research with Carl Rogers in the 1950s by studying the differences between successful and unsuccessful psychotherapy (Gendlin, 1969; Rogers, Gendlin, Kiesler, & Truax, 1967). Gendlin and his associates found that success in psychotherapy depended largely on what clients were doing and how they verbalized their problems. Whether or not a client would prove to be successful in therapy could be predicted well above chance on the basis of audiotapes of the first few therapy sessions as measured on the Experiencing Scale (Gendlin, Beebe, Cassens, Klein, and Oberlander, 1968; Gendlin & Tomlinson, 1967; Klein, Mathieu, Gendlin, & Kiesler, 1970). The Experiencing Scale (EXP Scale) measures the degree to which clients are attending to their experiencing as indicated by their verbal behavior.

Experiencing (Gendlin, 1962, 1981, 1984) refers to a client's immediately sensed but implicit experience. Implicit experience is typically sensed as a subtle, bodily feeling that involves vague meanings. The client feels "something" but does not yet know what it is.

The EXP Scale measures verbal behavior from low to high on a 7 point scale. The scale, which has high interrater reliability, is used by trained raters to rate tape-recorded segments of counseling interviews (Mathieu-Coughlan & Klein, 1984). At a low EXP level the client narrates events with no reference to present experiencing. At middle EXP levels the client can identify some emotions and may think about some personal connections to events but does not attend directly to his or her implicit sense of a situation. At high EXP levels the client refers to his or her experiencing, or subtle bodily sense of a situation.

Gendlin and his associates (Gendlin & Tomlinson, 1967; Klein et al., 1970) found that clients who were at lower levels of experiencing, as measured by the EXP Scale, tended to have unsuccessful outcomes in psychotherapy, whereas those who were above a certain level tended to be successful. This was established in a series of studies for neurotic individuals (Tomlinson & Hart, 1962; Walker, Rablen, & Rogers, 1960) and psychiatric inpatients (Gendlin, 1966; Rogers et al., 1967). Hinterkopf and Brunswick (1981) found similar results with psychiatric inpatients. More recent studies, summarized in Klein, Mathieu-Coughlan, and Kiesler (1986), have also found a correlation between EXP level and outcome. (However, it should be noted that a small percentage of those clients who are low on experiencing are nonetheless able to make progress in therapy [Durak, Bernstein, & Gendlin, 1997]. Also, a few case studies have been reported in which a client high in experiencing was unsuccessful in therapy [Leijssen, 1997]).

An important additional finding was that almost all unsuccessful clients, those at low EXP levels, did not increase their EXP level over the course of therapy. This means that they did not learn how to pay attention to subtle, inner, bodily feelings and so were not able to make good use of therapy. To overcome this problem Gendlin developed a method to teach unsuccessful clients to attend inside in this special way and so become more successful in therapy. He called this method *Focusing* (Gendlin, 1969, 1981). Research (Durak et al., 1997) has found that training in Focusing raises the experiencing level in therapy and contributes to therapeutic success.

What is it that almost all successful clients pay attention to? Gendlin had to develop a new term for that to which the successful clients give their attention. He called it a *felt sense.*

The Marvelous Felt Sense

In my workshops I frequently describe the felt sense in the following way (Hinterkopf, 1983, 1995a). The felt sense, the key concept in Focusing, is the vague, bodily, wholistic sense of a situation, such as a problem, creative project, or spiritual experiance. Focusing refers to a quiet, gentle, and powerful way of spending time with a felt sense to allow healing, insight, physical release, creative change, and spiritual growth to take place.

The felt sense is a wonderful phenomenon. It contains all of your inner knowing about a given situation and that which you do not yet know about yourself. Your felt sense can lead you to the next growth step. It can even sense an answer that has not yet been experienced (Gendlin, 1986). The felt sense is your sense of something before mind, body, and spirit are split apart.

Keeping an open attitude toward that which has not yet been experienced in a felt sense is frequently referred to as being open to the mystery of life. The felt sense helps you get in touch with your inner wisdom and hear the still, small voice within. It helps you experience your spiritual dimension.

Gendlin called the felt sense "felt" because you can feel it in your body. He called it "sense" because at first it is just a sense of something unclear and vague, not yet thought out, that has implicit meanings in it (see Figure 3.1). An example of a felt sense is the vague feeling you get when you leave your house and feel that you have forgotten something, but you don't know what. Another example of a felt sense is when you meet someone who seems nice to you on the surface, but for some unknown reason you get a vague, uncomfortable feeling about him or her. In this book I use the word *feeling* to refer to the felt sense.

It is important to attend to the vague, implicit felt sense, giving it an attitude of wondering curiosity. Often, staying with the felt sense until one has several words to describe it helps bring new meanings. Whereas successful clients stay with and pay attention to this vague feeling about a problem, unsuccessful clients only repeat that which they already know about an issue.

In the process of Focusing, the felt sense unfolds. As you attend to the felt sense, at least two parts become more clear:

Figure 3.1 Felt Sense Model

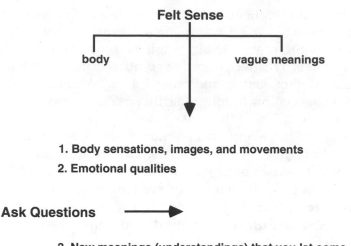

Felt Sense

body   vague meanings

1. **Body sensations, images, and movements**
2. **Emotional qualities**

Ask Questions ⟶

3. **New meanings (understandings) that you let come from the felt sense**

(a) body sensations, images, and movements; and (b) emotional qualities. Examples of body sensations are a heaviness in your chest or a pressure in your stomach. An example of a body image is getting a picture of a balloon that corresponds with the pressure in your stomach. An example of a body movement is jumping up and down because you are so excited. Although body sensations are essential in Focusing, body images and movements may or may not be present. A felt sense might also involve a sound or a smell.

Examples of emotional qualities are a heavy sadness, a feeling of emptiness, or a ball of anxiety. Emotional qualities are larger than single emotions because they have implicit meanings in them. There are only a limited number of emotions but an infinite number of emotional qualities. Whereas emotions give limited information, emotional qualities can give a vast amount of complex and subtle information about a situation.

After you have found just the right words to describe the felt sense, you can do a wonderful thing. You can ask open-ended "what" questions, such as, "What is it about this whole thing that leaves me feeling this way?" "What is the worst (or best) about this whole thing for me?" and "What does this whole thing need right now?"

In part three you then wait and *let* new meanings come to you from your felt sense.

For example, Joe may have a vague sense of uneasiness around his boss. He then asks the feeling, "What is it about this whole thing that leaves me feeling this way?" After several moments the meaning emerges, "He reminds me of my father." In this example the new meaning is a clarification of a situation. At other times the new meaning can be a solution to a problem or a correction of a mistaken belief.

The words that bring new meanings to you are different from words that you already know. The words that bring new meanings usually come more slowly and involve only a few words at a time. Often these words have an element of surprise. These words match the body sense and bring a physical feeling of relief or release with them. Examples of this kind of relief or release are when you remember the thing you forgot or realize why a seemingly nice person was bothering you. It may be painful to realize why you were feeling uncomfortable about a person, but there is a relief or release in realizing the truth of the matter. Gendlin calls this relief or release experience a *felt shift*.

When a person experiences a felt shift, psychospiritual growth occurs. The person is able to transcend his or her former frame of reference and is able to accept more parts of himself or herself, others, and life, at least in a small way. Because Focusing on a felt meaning usually produces a felt shift, it is a powerful tool for psychospiritual growth.

When a person is intellectualizing or rationalizing, he or she does not experience a felt shift. When a felt shift occurs, the person knows that new meanings have come from the felt sense. A release of the uncomfortable feeling indicates that the words authentically express that which is true inside. This means that noticing whether a felt shift has occurred is essential for authentic self-exploration and change in psychotherapy.

A felt shift may be subtle or dramatic. In its subtle form it might be realizing a new distinction or making a new connection. At times the felt sense can shift without the meaning having been totally clear. In its more dramatic form the felt shift has also been known as the moment of insight or the "aha!" experience. When a felt shift involves the transcendent dimension, psychospiritual growth takes place. Whether subtle or dramatic, the felt shift needs to be valued. It is important to take time to be with it to integrate it.

Example of Helping a Client Identify Parts of a Felt Sense

The following example illustrates how I helped a client identify different parts of a felt sense and suggested an open-ended "what" question, so that the felt sense could unfold into a felt shift. In this example the client has a spiritual experience as a result of Focusing on a felt sense.

Ms. D.'s daughter had lied to her a number of times in the recent past. Ms. D. said that she had been struggling with this issue for 3 days, and it had left her feeling miserable. She said it left her feeling hopeless, depressed, extremely tense, and at times, nauseated. (Hopeless and depressed were her emotions.)

To help her access her larger feeling or felt sense, I asked her, "How does this *whole* thing feel in your body?" (Use of the word "whole" in the question and asking Ms. D. to describe exactly how the whole issue felt in her body helped her become aware of her felt sense.) After a long pause she replied, "It feels tense all over, like something is clamping down on my stomach." ("Tense" was both a body sensation and an emotion. "Like something is clamping down on my stomach" is a body sensation with vague meanings in it.) I reflected her words by saying, "So it feels tense all over, like something is clamping down on your stomach." Then I suggested, "Perhaps you could stay with that feeling and notice if any other words come to describe the feeling." (I frequently give this suggestion to help a client stay with a felt sense a little longer.) After several moments she said, "It's strange, but it's like steps, mixed up steps, all over my body." I reflected these words by saying, "So it's like steps, mixed up steps, all over your body."

After about 15 seconds of silence I suggested, "Perhaps you could ask the feeling, 'What does this whole thing need?'" She waited several moments, paying attention to the feeling. Then, taking a deep breath, she said, "It needs giving the whole thing to God. I can now see the face of God, and I'm giving it to God." (This was a new, more explicit meaning.) I asked her how it felt in her body now, and she said that it felt a lot more relaxed and lighter. (This was a felt shift.) At this point I invited Ms. D. to take time to be with her new feeling. She then said, "It really helped me to have something concrete in my body to give to God. Before it was just swimming around in my head, all mixed up, and I couldn't give it to God, even though I wanted to."

In this example the client's spiritual experience involved vague, subtle, bodily feelings, at first "tense all over, like something clamping down on my stomach" and then, "like mixed-up steps all over my body." As the client paid attention to these feelings, they brought a new meaning: "It needs giving it to God." This new meaning was accompanied by an image: "I can now see the face of God." The transcendent growth process involved a physical release, a deep breath and a more relaxed, lighter feeling in her body. Ms. D. transcended her former frame of reference because she no longer had to solve the problem alone but could give it to God.

Implications for Practice

Notice the client's use of vague words, such as *like* and *like something*. Such words indicate that the client is paying attention to a vague feeling with unclear meanings or a felt sense. After the client said, "It feels tense all over, like something is clamping down on my stomach," some counselors would make the mistake of reflecting something too definite, possibly followed by a question. For example, they might say, "So you're feeling tense all over. Could it be that. . . ?" Instead, it is especially important to reflect all of the client's felt sense words, especially words that indicate lack of clarity, such as *like*, and invite the client to stay with the felt sense even longer (Hendricks, 1986).

Some clients have difficulty identifying emotions. Typically, I help such a client identify several major feelings, such as sadness, anger, fear, and joy, in their bodies. I might suggest that clients remember a sad time in their life, imagine themselves in that situation, and notice how the sadness feels in their body. For example, when one client remembered the time when his mother died, I asked him to describe his body sensations to me. He said he felt tears in his eyes, a lump in his throat, and a heaviness in his chest. I then had him remember times when he felt anger, fear, and joy.

Some clients may be able to identify emotions mentally but have difficulty locating emotions in their body. These people may also

23

need help before learning to Focus. I explain that the emotions that we *think* we have may be different from the emotions that we *actually* have in our bodies. As an example I tell them that I might think I am disappointed about a loss, but when I check in my body, I might actually be angry about the loss. It is the anger that is actually bothering me and giving my body stress.

The reason for continually identifying bodily feelings by asking, "How does that whole thing feel in your body now?" is that these subtle bodily feelings are a source of wisdom. In Focusing the term *body* means body, mind, and soul experienced together. Some religious traditions refer to this as heart. Gendlin (1996) explained that the human organism is marvelously complex; it knows far more than we can consciously think at any given time. He says that this is not the body that is reduced to physiology, but rather a body from out of which living happens. It is always implicitly intricate; it includes a whole range of possible experiences that have never happened but could come.

The felt sense is implicitly contextual. It takes other people and our environment into account (Gendlin, 1996). It leads us to larger and larger wholes. Spiritually, the felt sense tells us what is needed in a culture-free way, whether it be more separation from or more unity with others. The felt sense helps us stay in touch with a pro-life energy that we sometimes call '"spirit."

Conclusion

In this chapter, research supporting Focusing has been cited to show that attention to experiencing is generally necessary for success in psychotherapy. Although therapy alone does not usually raise experiencing level, that level can be raised by teaching clients to attend to their felt sense through Focusing training. When clients attend to their felt sense and it unfolds into a felt shift in which a transcendent growth process occurs, the experience may be considered spiritual.

CHAPTER

4

Focusing Attitudes

As part of the Focusing Method, I have taught clients the importance of keeping a number of attitudes while attending to feelings (Hinterkopf, 1983). These attitudes are crucial to the Focusing process. When clients experience difficulty focusing, it is frequently because they are having difficulty keeping one or more of the Focusing attitudes toward their feelings (felt senses). At such times the counselor can remind the client to adopt the needed attitude. Remembering to keep the attitudes allows feelings to be in process and change. This in turn allows the psychospiritual growth process to take place.

In this chapter I describe the following Focusing attitudes: (a) keeping a receptive attitude; (b) keeping an expectant attitude; (c) keeping a patient attitude; and (d) keeping an accepting, friendly attitude. Suggestions for helping clients learn these attitudes are given. A case example illustrates how teaching these attitudes in counseling can help facilitate spiritual growth.

Keeping a Receptive Attitude

Keeping a receptive attitude means letting the answers emerge rather than agonizing to find solutions or trying to control the solutions. Focusing does not involve obsessing or associating. Sometimes when clients seem to be trying to figure out an answer, I suggest that they temporarily report only what they notice below their necks in their bodies. When clients are keeping a receptive attitude, they frequently have the experience of having new meanings come without mental effort. They find that these meanings are steps toward solutions.

Keeping an Expectant Attitude

Keeping an open, curious attitude means expecting that there is more to learn about an issue if a feeling about an issue is present. An expectant attitude may be contrasted to thinking that one already knows everything there is to know about an issue. A client having a closed attitude might say, "This is all there is to this problem." Such a closed attitude can keep a client from being open to new meanings that emerge from the felt sense.

Keeping a Patient Attitude

Keeping a patient attitude means accepting the timing in which feelings change and new meanings or answers are revealed. Although answers usually come during the Focusing process, sometimes they do not come until later. When clients are impatient with their feelings, I sometimes suggest that they remember areas in their life in which they are patient, sense how it feels to have such a patient attitude, and adopt such an attitude toward their feelings. For example, if a client is patient in working on automobiles, I might suggest that they adopt the same kind of patience with their feelings.

Keeping an Accepting, Friendly Attitude

Keeping an accepting, friendly attitude means keeping radical acceptance toward everything that emerges in one's process. Some clients find it strange and difficult to be friendly toward something painful. For example, a client may be angry and frustrated with his pain. Then it is important to make a separate, accepting space for the anger and frustration and also a protected space for the painful felt sense. So instead of attacking the felt sense, the client learns that even a painful felt sense has important information for living. If clients are having difficulty keeping an accepting, friendly attitude, I sometimes suggest that they imagine how they would treat someone else, such as a friend or a hurt child, with a similar problem. They are then usually able to keep a more friendly attitude toward their felt sense.

Example of Keeping the Focusing Attitudes

The following example shows how reminding a client to keep the Focusing attitudes helps bring about a felt shift. Focusing therapy is frequently distinguished by the attitude of being friendly and compassionate toward all bodily experience. When the counselor notices that a client is not being accepting toward some inner bodily experience, the client is invited to try out such an attitude.

Mr. J., a 38-year-old male, said that he wanted to Focus on his weight problem. I asked him how his weight problem felt in his body. He said that the problem had several feelings including feeling flushed in the face, tense in the neck, bloated in the stomach, and tingling in the hands. He reported that he was sad because he saw himself as a gunny sack bulging with potatoes.

After helping him adopt a kind attitude toward his sadness, I asked him, "How would this whole thing feel if you had a friendly attitude toward it?" He said that it was difficult to imagine a friendly attitude toward the part of himself that wanted to overeat because he felt so ashamed of it. I asked him, "Could you imagine creating one place for your shame and another place for the part of you that wants to overeat?" He said that he could do this. Then I asked him if he could imagine having a friendly, kind attitude toward someone else with the same type of weight problem. After imagining this, he was able to adopt a friendly attitude toward the part that wanted to overeat. He then reported feeling more relaxed and having more energy to do something about his weight problem. He said that he realized that he had been trying to exert too much control over this part of himself by keeping it hidden. In a later session he reported, "Remembering to keep a friendly attitude towards my weight problem has made taking action to lose weight almost easy."

This example illustrates how blocks to action (in this case the client's block to losing weight) are frequently released when these parts are carefully listened to in a compassionate Focusing manner. Self criticism often holds these blocks in place. Adopting an accepting attitude toward the feelings (in this case both the sadness and the shame) frequently releases the block.

This example is spiritual in nature because the client was able to attend to a subtle, bodily feeling with vague meanings that brought new, clearer meanings involving a transcendent growth process. Mr. J.'s subtle, bodily feeling with vague meanings involved an image of a gunny sack bulging with potatoes and his feeling flushed in the face, tense in the neck, bloated in the stomach, tingling in the hands, and sad. A new, clearer meaning was his realization that he had been trying to exert too much control over this part of himself by keeping it hidden. The client's experience involved a transcendent growth process because the client was able to have a more compassionate attitude than he previously had for the part of himself that wanted to overeat.

Conclusion

The example in this chapter illustrates how attitudes taught in Focusing help facilitate psychospiritual growth. Campbell and McMahon (1985) have referred to adopting these attitudes as creating a "caring-feeling presence." It involves being genuinely interested and at the same time nonintruding. The counselor needs to model these attitudes toward the client. At times, the client can be helped to remember and feel a time when he or she experienced kindness, tenderness, and caring. When a client is able to create a caring, feeling presence for the distressing places within, the psychospiritual process is allowed to unfold.

CHAPTER

Keeping a Certain Distance

Clients often make one of two mistakes when working on a problem. Either they are too close to a problem, usually by being overwhelmed by emotions, or they are too far away from a problem, usually by intellectualizing about it. I have found it important to teach clients to find a certain distance (Hinterkopf, 1983): close enough to feel the problem in their body, but far enough away from it to realize that their life is greater than the problem. The appropriate distance from a problem is the distance at which clients can process material and realize change. At this distance, clients experience some relief or release. They work through problems most frequently when they are able to keep this distance.

When clients are too close to a problem, they usually feel much discomfort regarding that problem. They usually look uncomfortable, and they may say, "I feel overwhelmed," "This whole thing is weighing me down," or "I feel engulfed, like I'm drowning in it." When clients are too distant, they usually sound flat or nonemotional, and they might say, "Maybe there's something there," "I'm having trouble feeling anything," or "I don't feel anything." Although everyone experiences being too close or too distant at times, some clients tend to be too close or too distant for long periods of time. Other clients alternate between being too close and too distant.

Helping clients to keep a certain distance frequently helps them move in a direction of higher and broader scope and experience the spiritual dimension. Learning to keep a certain distance helps clients to develop an observer self. It is the observer self that is able to see the whole problem from a distance. Counselors can facilitate the psychospiritual growth process by noticing when clients are too close or too distant from a problem. They can then make certain Focusing suggestions to help clients find the best distance.

In this chapter finding a certain distance in Focusing will be related to the spiritual wellness model. Finding a certain distance can help both clients who are in spiritual emergency and in spiritual repression return to a more centered position from which they can experience spiritual development. Instructions to help clients keep a certain distance are presented and illustrated with examples.

The Spiritual Wellness Model and a Certain Distance

The spiritual wellness model presented in chapter 1 can be related to finding a certain distance (see Figure 5.1)

Clients who are too close to their feelings and preoccupied with spiritual content to the detriment of wellness in other areas of their life are in spiritual emergency. In this situation clients need to find more distance from their feelings to allow for spiritual development or spiritual process. Clients who are too distant from their feelings regarding spiritual content may be seen as being in spiritual repression. In this situation clients need to connect with their feelings to allow for spiritual development. Each of these situations are discussed in more detail below.

Spiritual Emergency

These clients are usually overwhelmed by distressing feelings and preoccupied with spiritual content to the detriment of other dimensions of wellness. In the following example, using the Focusing principle of finding a certain distance helps ground and center the client and helps him work through issues involving spiritual emergency.

Mr. R. came to see me because he was preoccupied with thoughts that another soul had taken over his body. He felt overpowered by an overwhelming energy that he called

Figure 5.1 Spiritual Wellness and Certain Distance Model

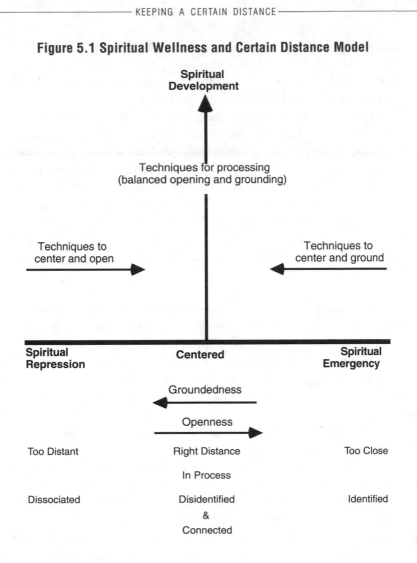

Note. Adapted from Chandler, C. K., Holden, J. M., & Kolander, C. A. (1992). Counseling for spiritual wellness: Theory and practice. *Journal of Counseling and Development,* vol. 71, p. 170. Copyright 1992. Reprinted by permission.

Kundalini energy. He experienced the overwhelming energy in his penis and in his heart. When I asked him to describe the energy, he said it felt like he would burst with energy, and it caused extreme discomfort. His extreme discomfort indicated that he needed more distance. I suggested that he might imagine himself as a neutral reporter who could describe the energy to me. He said that the energy was so overpowering that it felt like another being had walked into his body. It felt and looked like a balloon ready to burst.

At this point I thought he had enough distance, so I suggested that he ask, "What in my life feels like this uncomfortable energy?" After many moments of silence he said he was getting an image of sucking on another man's penis. He realized that this energy had to do with his bisexuality, a fact that he didn't like to admit. The energy in his heart had to do with his love for women. I then asked him how the whole thing felt in his body now, and he said that the energy had calmed down and he felt relaxed, as though he were in a bed of light.

In this example, finding more distance from his overpowering energy helped Mr. R. become more centered. This, along with describing the feeling in his body and asking the Focusing question, "What in my life feels like this?" helped ground him. After finding the right distance, he could realize new connections between the overwhelming energy and his bisexuality. At this distance he could experience his spirituality because he was able to accept more parts or aspects of himself. His spiritual experience resulted in more calm and being in a bed of light.

In using this example I do not mean to imply that difficult tasks, such as acknowledging one's bisexuality, can be dealt with in one brief session. The client had done previous work on this issue. A client usually needs many Focusing sessions to change an attitude about a major life issue. However, in this session the client was able to accept his bisexuality at a deeper level. Rather than accepting his bisexuality only mentally, Mr. R. said that he was able to accept it more in his body, with his whole being. This was a step of real change.

In my practice I have repeatedly seen clients who are overwhelmed by distressing feelings return to a state of equilibrium in a matter of minutes when I help them find more distance. Some clients sustain their equilibrium; others need help several times before being able to maintain a certain distance.

Clients who are too close to their feelings but not in spiritual emergency might be at a less extreme position on the horizontal dimension in the spiritual wellness model. These clients are usually identified with their emotions. They can readily describe their emotions, but these uncomfortable emotions are repeated over and over, resulting in dead ends (Gendlin, 1996). Such a client might say, "I'm afraid that God will punish me. I don't know what it's about, but I'm always afraid." or "I feel angry at God all the time." Usually such clients can be helped by noticing how the emotion feels in their body and observing their feeling from a distance. This helps them disidentify with the emotion while still remaining connected to it.

Spiritual Repression

At the other extreme of the horizontal dimension of the spiritual wellness model is spiritual repression. These clients are usually dissociated from their feelings and have too much distance. In dissociation, clients *automatically* split off from their feelings and cannot feel their emotions, even when they wish to do so. (Clients at the right distance, who are able to observe themselves, have a choice to feel or not feel their feelings.) Too distant or dissociated clients may have many sophisticated interpretations and inferences for their predicaments but no experiential process (Gendlin, 1996). Such clients may say, "I've been religious all my life, but I've never experienced my relationship with God." They might say that they can't feel anything or that they feel very little. Work with these clients involves helping them connect with their feelings and usually takes longer than work with clients who are too close to their feelings.

Helping Clients When They Are Too Close or Too Distant

Two moves that tend to help most clients—both those who are too close and those who are too distant—find a better distance to problems are saying hello to a problem and "ittification" (Cornell, 1996). First, I might make the following suggestion to a client about saying hello to a problem: "You might try saying, 'Hello, I know you are there,' or 'I see you are there.'" This usually helps the uncomfortable feeling ease up a bit. It is a way of acknowledging that it feels the way it does. It suggests that the client is willing to become a good listener to the part that feels bad.

Second, in suggesting ittification, I use the words *it, part,* or a *place* to help the client create the right relationship or distance (Cornell, 1990). For example:

C: I feel scared.
T: So there's a part of you that feels scared.
Or:
C: I feel depressed.
T: There's a place in you that feels depressed.
Or:
C: There's a pressure—moving up in my chest.
T: There's a pressure and you feel it moving up in your chest.

Both saying hello and ittification help clients learn to find a certain distance and realize that there is a part of them that is able to observe the problem along with the uncomfortable feelings.

Helping Clients When They Are Too Close

Many clients in therapy are in such extreme discomfort, especially when they are overwhelmed by a problem, that they need more specific guidance to find a certain distance. To help clients find more distance, I might offer parts or all of the following explanation:

> If you feel too close to a problem, you can find more distance by visualizing the problem at a distance. When you imagine setting the whole problem at some distance, an image will frequently come to you. For example, if you felt upset about an argument that you had with your boss, you might get an image of yourself and your boss arguing. You could take this image along with all the feelings connected with it and imagine setting it in the corner of the room until you could see around the edges of it. Sometimes putting a problem in a picture frame helps contain it.
>
> You will find that different problems need to be imagined at different distances. Some problems need more distance than others. For example, some problems may need to be placed next to you and some down the block or in the next state or country. At times you may find it helpful to imagine that you are a neutral observer seeing yourself with the problem and the feelings about the problem at some distance. When you are far enough away from a problem, you will feel less overwhelmed and more able to work on the problem.

Examples of Helping Clients When They Are Too Close

Mr. N., who was dealing with a history of shoplifting, reported that he was having difficulty experiencing God's forgiveness even though he was no longer shoplifting. During the counseling session I asked him how the whole shoplifting issue felt in his body. He said that it felt very heavy and guilty with sadness in it.

Because he looked overwhelmed, I asked if he could set this issue out at some distance to see the whole thing. He imagined putting the whole thing into a picture on the wall. He then said that he could see many things involved in it, including anger at his parents for placing more importance on acquiring money than on loving him. He could understand how his shoplifting was understandable when seen in a larger context: It had been *his* distorted way of placing great importance on money. He had thought he could save money by shoplifting. As he saw his problem from this new perspective, he experienced a felt shift. He reported feeling that a great weight had been lifted and that he was now able to experience God's forgiveness.

By finding the right distance to his problem the client was able to experience spiritual growth. He was able to transcend his former frame of reference by having understanding and compassion for a previously rejected part of himself, namely the injured part of himself that had been involved in shoplifting.

Some clients, who have more difficulty in finding a certain distance, need several suggestions to help them find the appropriate distance. In the next example I try several different ways of helping the client find more distance. I combine finding more distance in T2 and T3 with suggestions for adopting a friendly attitude in T4 and T5.

Mr. J., a successful public speaker, contacted me because he started having panic attacks while he was giving speeches. He explained that the panic attacks were overwhelming and paralyzing. Until recently he had a self-concept of himself as "superman." He saw himself as a strong, clear, dynamic speaker. When he had a panic attack, it felt as though he was zapped with "kryptonite" that drained him of his energy.

T1: So you could say hello to that part of you that feels pan-icked about public speaking. (Silence of 40 seconds) How does this whole thing feel in your body now?

C1: I feel a weakness and a jitteriness in my chest, especially in my shoulders, arms, and nerves. They feel like guitar strings that have been strung too tight. I feel a terrifying drain of my energy. I'm paralyzed with fear—frozen. There's a constricted breathing in my chest, like hyperventilating, like death.

T2: I wonder if you could imagine putting this whole panic attack out at a distance?

C2: That seems too hard to do.

T3: Perhaps you could become a neutral observer of your-self, like a reporter, seeing yourself at a distance with the panic attack. You can describe it to me whenever you're ready.

C3: (30-second silence) I see myself at a park, walking too close to a fire and getting burned. It's scary. I feel better, but I still feel weak and helpless. (The client said this in a self-critical tone of voice.)

T4: Then it seems especially important that you create a friendly, accepting place for your weak and helpless feelings.

C4: (35-second silence) That seems really hard to do. I don't think I've ever accepted that part of myself.

T5: I wonder if you could imagine how you would be toward a friend who had panic attacks while he was speaking publicly.

C5: Yeah, that works. I would be understanding and empathic with a friend who had panic attacks while he was speak-ing publicly. It feels better now. Now I see myself in a wooded park by a pond and it feels more peaceful and still.

The suggestions in T1, T2, and T3 help the client find more distance and develop an observer self. In C3 he is able to see him-self in a park, walking too close to a fire, but feeling somewhat better. Because he seemed self-critical, I gave additional sugges-tions to adopt a friendly, accepting attitude in T4 and T5. This results in the client finding the right distance in C5. His feelings change. He now feels peaceful and still. At a later time the client reported that his panic attacks had ceased after this session.

While clients typically need to find the right distance when they are overwhelmed with uncomfortable feelings, it may not be appropriate to help the client find more distance immediately. If clients are expressing emotions, such as crying or expressing anger, it is usually important that the counselor let them express these feelings before trying to help them find the right distance.

If clients have been sexually or otherwise physically abused, it may be important for them to choose a signal before Focusing to indicate that they wish to stop the Focusing process. Such signals may be needed if they are unable to express that they feel too overwhelmed to continue the process. They may need to stop their Focusing process temporarily and possibly receive more instruction about finding the right distance.

Helping Clients When They Are Too Distant

Clients who are too distant from their feelings seldom come to counseling on their own because they rarely feel the discomfort that motivates people to enter therapy. However, sometimes such people come for therapy on their own or at the request of their partner. Other clients may be too distant only some of the time.

To help clients when they are too distant connect with their feelings, I might offer some of the following suggestions.

- If you feel too distant from a problem, you may not want to set a problem out at a distance. You can keep the problem inside of you and notice the whole thing.
- Be accepting of yourself no matter what you feel or don't feel. At first, you might try noticing only what you feel below your neck. Notice any sensations in your body. Don't worry about whether they are felt senses or not. You might try talking about the worst problem in your life. If you feel anything, slow down, acknowledge it, and report it.
- If you have difficulty feeling a problem, you might try making a hypothetical statement to elicit feelings. You might pick an issue and say to your body, "I feel perfectly wonderful about this whole issue," or you might try saying, "I feel completely glorious about how my life is going." Then notice if any feelings arise in you.

- Some people who have difficulty feeling a problem find it useful to ask how their "inner child" feels about the problem. They find it more acceptable for their inner child, rather than the adult part of themselves, to have vulnerable feelings. If this is helpful for you, you might try asking yourself, "How does my inner child feel about this whole issue today?"

In the following example the client is initially dissociated from his feelings.

Example of Helping a Too-Distant Client

Father B., an elderly priest, came to see me because he had never experienced God. I spent months helping him experience sensations in his body. At first he had only a slight twinge in his knee or a small ache in his elbow. Sometimes he reported feeling "nothing inside." Then he said he had a vague, overall sadness. One day he came in with a book on personal growth and said, "This inner child stuff really spoke to me." That day I asked him how his inner child was feeling, and he was able to describe how he felt in some detail. Later in the session he could describe how his experience of God felt in his body.

At a less extreme position on the horizontal dimension of spiritual repression, but still too distant from feelings, are clients who can verbalize emotions that they think they have, but they have difficulty identifying these emotions in their bodies. With such clients, I might briefly describe where in my own body I feel different emotions. This helps them identify their own bodily feelings, which are sometimes different from their preconceived emotions.

Ms. K. seemed to have a happy demeanor that was not grounded. She told me that God had been good to her and that she was a very lucky person. I asked her how all of that felt in her body. After waiting for several moments, tears came to her eyes. She said that there was still a lot of grief about her husband who had died almost a year before.

After becoming connected to her bodily feelings, Ms. K. was able to process her feelings of grief and have bodily felt spiritual experiences. Her nonverbal expression became more congruent with her verbal expression.

Conclusion

This chapter has shown how finding a certain distance may be used to help both clients who are in spiritual emergency and in spiritual repression return to a more centered position from which they can experience spiritual development. Finding a certain distance may be combined with adopting the Focusing attitudes (as seen in the example of Mr. J.) to create conditions that allow the felt sense to unfold into a felt shift. When clients have been assisted in regaining process, spiritual experiences are more likely to occur. In the next chapter the problem of clients whose inner critics keep them from being in process is addressed.

CHAPTER

Focusing and the Inner Critic

C lients often experience what Gendlin (1981) has called the "critic." The critic often seems like a voice inside or just outside a person's head that says, "You're no good," "You're stupid," "What you're feeling is wrong," or "What you're trying to do will probably fail." The critic is usually experienced as coming "at me" rather than coming "from me." It absorbs some of the characteristics of one's actual parents, but it is usually more destructive and irrational than one's parents ever were. As a result of critic attacks clients frequently feel pain, confusion, and fear. Some clients may not experience the critic as having words but only as a vaguely bad feeling (Gendlin, 1996).

At times negative feelings, such as guilt and fear, may be healthy and even growth-producing. However, the critic tends to inhibit psycho-spiritual growth. In particular, the critic often blocks the Focusing process. Focusing brings physiological release and more life energy, but the critic brings more tension, constriction, heaviness, and dullness.

Because the critic can block growth, the counselor needs to be alert to note when clients are experiencing a growth-inhibiting critic. At such times counselors can help their clients resume the psychospiritual change process by using various interventions or approaches. When these interventions help bring about a felt shift, clients may report being more open to their spirituality. Intervening to deal with the critic when clients are discussing religious and spiritual issues is especially important because for many people religion is experienced, at least partly, as a series of critical voices.

This chapter presents three approaches to help counselors work with clients' inner critics. These approaches can be used to identify, transform, and integrate inner critics for clients' benefit.

Different clients need different approaches to their critics, and the same client may need different approaches at different times. Whatever approach is used, it is important that the client experience a felt difference of easing as a result of an intervention. If the client does not feel some relief, expansion, and more life energy, a different approach may be needed.

Three approaches I have found useful in helping clients work with their inner critics are (a) distinguishing Focusing from the inner critic (Hinterkopf, 1985a), (b) finding a stronger position than the critic (Young, 1994), and (c) Focusing on a felt sense associated with the critic (Hinterkopf, 1985b). Clients who are frequently overwhelmed by their critics may need the help of their counselors to implement the first two approaches before moving to the third approach.

Distinguishing Focusing From the Inner Critic

Clients who feel overwhelmed by their critics usually experience themselves as victims of their critics. These clients often find the first approach, learning to distinguish the critic from that which comes from their Focusing process, an essential first step in learning to work with their critics. Many of these clients find it difficult to remember a time when they did not feel anxiety or depression as a result of their critics. When their critics become active, such clients frequently feel helpless and unable to change.

When the critic blocks the psychospiritual growth process in counseling, clients need to learn to recognize the critic and distinguish it from the experience of Focusing. Clients who are unable to distinguish the difference between Focusing and the critic may be afraid to explore inside because they are afraid that they will only become more anxious or depressed as a result of increased awareness of the critic. Other clients are confused in their thinking about their critics and may take their critics at face value. These clients may feel terrorized by their inner critics.

On several occasions when I have taught suicidal clients differences between Focusing and the critic, they have exclaimed that it was the critic they were trying to kill in their suicide attempt. Death seemed better than having to continue to live with a relentlessly nagging, mean, and destructive inner enemy and the feelings that resulted from its influence. Helping these clients distinguish Focusing from the critic frequently enabled them to take the first steps in building a healthy, life-affirming sense of self.

I have found that the following list of contrasting qualities helps clients distinguish between what comes from Focusing and what comes from the critic. This list also helps counselors identify when their clients are reacting to an inner critic and when they are Focusing.

Focusing	The Critic
Brings easing and more life energy	Brings tension, dullness, and constriction
From deep inside	From inside or just outside a person's head
From me	At me
Still, small voice	Chatters
Whispers	Nags (repetitive)
Leads	Drives
Encourages	Discourages
In the present	In the past or future
Leads to hope	Leads to depression
Brings peace	Brings fear and anxiety
Specific	Overgeneralized
Personal	Impersonal
Creative	Destructive
Kind, neutral	Mean, cruel

I frequently explain these differences to clients as follows: The major distinction between Focusing and the critic is that Focusing *brings easing and more life energy* that leads to forward living, whereas the critic *brings tension, dullness, and constriction*. Focusing makes you feel more caring and open to others and to life, but the critic makes you constrict and withdraw from others and life.

What comes from Focusing usually seems to come *from deep inside*. The critic's words usually seem to come *from our heads or just outside our heads*. Gendlin has said that what comes from Focusing is experienced as *from me*, whereas the critic is experienced as *at me*.

I find it useful to refer to what comes from Focusing as the *still, small voice*. Judeo-Christian people frequently identify what comes from Focusing as a way that God, Christ, or the Holy Spirit reveals itself to them. The critic often *chatters, nags, and repeats itself relentlessly*. The critic often uses the words *must, ought,* and *should*, frequently, in what seems to be a loud tone of voice. The words that come from Focusing usually come slowly and just a few at a time. Focusing *leads* us with life-forward energy from our center, whereas the critic usually *drives*.

The Focusing voice *encourages* us, even when it encourages us to make major changes in our life; the critic usually *discourages* us. For example, the critic might discourage and drive us by calling us names such as stupid, bad, selfish, or irresponsible. At times like this, you may find it useful to ask, "What is it I really want to do in this situation?" and "What would bring easing?" For example, if your critic is telling you that you are stupid and irresponsible because you aren't getting a task done on time, you might ask yourself what you really want to do in this situation. In reply you might receive the encouraging answer that you would feel better and you could relax more if you finished the task on time.

What comes from Focusing is *in the present*. You will learn what you need to do right now. The critic is often *in the past or future*. The critic may tell you to feel bad about something you can't change in the past or to worry about something over which you have no control in the future.

Whereas focusing *leads to hope,* the critic often *leads to depression*. Focusing can help you create new possibilities, but the critic can negate possibilities. Whereas Focusing *brings* a sense of *peace,* the critic often *brings fear and anxiety*.

What comes from Focusing is usually *specific* and *personal;* the critic is often *overgeneralized* and *impersonal*. For example, the Focusing voice might specify your next step. On the other hand, the critic might say, "*All* people should be good." or "You should *always* be polite." The critic is frequently simplistic. The felt sense in Focusing has an intricate and unique sense of a problem or issue.

What comes from Focusing is *creative* and brings more life; what comes from the critic is usually *destructive* of life. This includes both physical and psychological life.

Whereas the Focusing voice speaks in a *kind* or *neutral* manner, the critic often speaks in a *mean* or *cruel* manner.

The nonverbal signs that clients give are often clues as to whether they are reacting to a critic or whether they are experiencing Focusing. For example, two different clients may get the words, "Let go and let God." One client, experiencing Focusing, may say these words with a smile that brings more relaxation to her body. Her tightly crossed arms and legs become uncrossed, and the muscles in her face and body become more relaxed. For this person, the words come from her Focusing process. The other client, reacting to an inner critic, may say the same words, but his face becomes tighter. His jaw becomes more clenched. His crossed arms and legs become more tightly crossed. Muscles in his face and body become more constricted.

These nonverbal signs are important in working with religious material because they frequently indicate whether religious material was experienced as abusive or growth producing. For example, when a client says, "God is all powerful" or "I need to trust God," it is important for the counselor to check the client's resulting inner experience to see if the words brought more easing or more constriction. To do this, the counselor can ask the client, "When you say those words, how does it feel inside?" If the client replies that the words brought more constriction, the counselor might ask, "I wonder if those words are coming from your inner critic?"

Example of Distinguishing

The following example shows how a client is helped by learning the difference between what comes from Focusing and what comes from the inner critic.

> Ms. W., a 27-year-old single mother who had recently been divorced, came to see me because of her depression. She said that God was telling her to throw herself in front of a car and kill herself. She reported that she felt very tense and anxious when she heard these words. (As we talked, it became clear that she was not experiencing auditory hallucinations, but that these words were forming inside her head.)
>
> After discussing her guilt about the divorce and her limitations in the marriage, I explained some of the distinctions between Focusing and the inner critic. I said that I believed God wanted us to have more life and I thought that the words about killing herself were coming from her inner critic.

She agreed and said that she had been raised to believe in a harsh, punitive God. A look of relief came to her face and her body relaxed. In the next session she reported feeling less depressed because she no longer believed that God was telling her to kill herself.

After the client learned to identify and distinguish her inner critic from her Focusing process, she was able to regain her ability to process material about her divorce. She was able to pay attention to implicit feelings and let them unfold into explicit meanings. No longer taking her inner critic at face value, she was able to accept the part of herself that could not tolerate the marriage and needed to get divorced.

Finding a Stronger Position Than the Critic

Clients who see themselves as smaller than their critics and tend to feel powerless in the face of their critics often find the second approach, finding a stronger position than the critic, to be helpful and life-giving (Young, 1994). This approach, in which a client is taught to find a stronger position than the critic, includes setting the critic out in front of oneself, seeing it at a distance than oneself, and asking, "How would I feel if I didn't have this critic?" The next example illustrates how I helped a client feel stronger than her inner critic.

Example of Finding a Stronger Position Than the Critic

Ms. M., who was a counselor herself, had a keen awareness of her inner critic but still felt debilitated by it at times. She reported that she sometimes spent hours feeling terrorized by her critic.

I asked her where she experienced her critic, and she said that it was located in the back of her head to the right. I then asked her what her critic would look like if she could get an image of it. She answered that it would look like her father, who had verbally abused her. Because she looked extremely uncomfortable as we talked, I asked her how big her father was in relationship to her. She replied that he looked twice as big as she did. I suggested that she move her critic in front of her at a distance at eye-level or lower until her critic was only half her size or smaller. Ms. M. did this and became somewhat more relaxed.

I then asked her, "Is there a place you could imagine putting your critic so he can't attack you?" She said that he needed to be put into a trunk with a good lock on it. I asked her how she would feel if her critic, who looked like her father, were locked in the trunk. She replied, "I would feel a lot lighter and more energetic." The client looked more relaxed, had more color in her face, and sat more upright.

Ms. M. was then able to process her sadness about feeling victimized for many years. In the next session she reported that the idea of making her father visually smaller than herself and placing him in an enclosed place where he could not attack her helped her between sessions.

During the Focusing process a client frequently becomes more aware of irrational assumptions made by the critic. In addition to using the Focusing approach with a client's critic, interventions from other therapies may be applied. For example, interventions from cognitive-behavioral therapy, rational-emotive therapy, Gestalt, neurolinguistic programming, and Transactional Analysis may be helpful. Any of these interventions can be made more powerful by checking the client's felt sense before and after an intervention to see if it has brought more relief, release, and easing (Gendlin, 1996).

Focusing on a Felt Sense Associated With an Inner Critic

Clients who are overwhelmed by their critics often need time to learn the first two approaches of working with the critic before learning the third approach, Focusing on a felt sense associated with a critic. On the other hand, people who have a certain distance from their critics and are not constantly overwhelmed by them may find the first two approaches unnecessary.

Ultimately, the inner critic needs to be owned, transformed, and integrated. The third approach to working with the critic, Focusing on a felt sense associated with a critic, is used to help clients integrate their critics. The third approach might involve (a) Focusing on the critic, (b) Focusing on the whole relationship between critic and victim, or (c) Focusing on one's felt sense as the critic arises.

Focusing on the Critic

To Focus on the critic, the client needs to be able to experience the critic from the inside. A client overwhelmed by his or her critic usually experiences the critic as attacking from the outside. To experience the critic from the inside, the client may need to imagine how it would feel to be inside the critic. The client may then Focus on this feeling.

> Ms. L. had an inner critic who continued to attack her about a mistake she had made, even after she had worked on the issue using cognitive therapy. I suggested that she might ask herself, "How would I feel if I were the critic part of me?" The client slowly became aware of a felt sense of an angry-around-the-edges critic being jumpy and fearful inside. As she continued to Focus on these feelings, she realized that this part of her needed love and respect. I asked her how it would feel if she, as the critic part, imagined receiving love and respect. She waited several moments and reported that she felt warm, peaceful, and glowing. She then realized that the critic had a good motive in wanting to help her do better. Several sessions later she reported that Focusing as if she were the critic had had a lasting effect, indicating that her transformed critic was more integrated with the rest of her personality.

Focusing on the Whole Relationship Between Critic and Victim

When clients are identified with being victims of their inner critics, I have found it useful to help them Focus on the whole relationship between critic and victim. This can help bring about a healing transformation.

The first step is to notice how each part feels. The second step is to notice and feel both parts together at the same time. Cornell and McGavin (1996) have called this move "Standing It." The term helps remind clients that they need to stand the tension, discomfort, and ambiguity of feeling both parts at the same time. The third step is patiently waiting for something new to emerge.

> Ms. Q., who had made much progress in working on her critic, said that she still had periods of several hours when she felt

victimized by her inner critic, especially when she was ill. After she told me about her last episode with her critic, I suggested that she get a felt sense of each part, her victim part and her critic part. She said that the two parts felt like they had different energies. The victim part felt weak and fearful. The critic part felt like frantic, agitated, erratic, energy, often giving her double messages.

I suggested that she see and feel both the critic and the victim parts of herself at a distance and notice the whole relationship between them. She reported that when the critic became active, the victim part would collapse and cower in fear. I then asked her, "If you could feel both the victim part and the critic part at the same time, how would the whole thing feel?" She waited several moments and then in a surprised tone of voice said that it felt like a strong energy rising up inside of her.

After this session the client reported that her critic no longer had power over her. She noticed an increase of energy in many areas of her life.

Focusing on One's Felt Sense as the Critic Arises

As the client becomes less oppressed by the critic, the counselor may not need to use the previous interventions described in this chapter. In this case, I give mostly empathic listening responses, carefully reflecting felt sense words exactly. The following excerpt from a client's session gives such an example.

C: I'm sensing a hurt little girl inside. (Pause) She seems to be hiding in a cave.

T: So you're sensing that there's a hurt little girl inside who seems to be hiding in a cave.

C: Yes, I want to be sure to love and protect her. (Pause) So she can come out into the sunshine and laugh and play. (Long pause) Yes, that feels better.

T: So now she can come out into the sunshine and laugh and play.

C: (Long pause) And now there's this amorphous power covered with slime. Ugh. (Pause) It's very powerful, and sometimes I get afraid of it. It's sort of like a monster that can criticize me.

49

T: So, there's this amorphous power covered with slime that sometimes scares you and can criticize you.

C: Yeah, but now I see that it needs to come out into the light too—out there with the little girl. (Long pause) It needs to be tempered with compassion, so it can become a good power. (Long pause) Yes, that feels really good now—full of energy and light!

Making an intervention with this client's inner critic in this session would probably distract the client from her process. Different aspects of the client, including her inner critic, are naturally being transformed and integrated. She finds my presence and empathic listening responses helpful and sufficient.

This example illustrates the creative, nonrational, nonlinear nature of the Focusing process. One counselor said that Focusing often involves surprises, material that cannot be anticipated. In this sense Focusing is an adventure. An adventure has a general goal, but involves movement into the unknown. Therein lies both the uncertainty for the counselor, who guides the process but does not control the outcome, and the excitement for the counselor, who is often surprised and delighted by the outcome.

Conclusion

In this chapter three approaches to help clients identify, transform, and integrate their inner critics have been presented: (a) distinguishing Focusing from the inner critic, (b) finding a stronger position than the critic, and (c) Focusing on a felt sense associated with the critic. These three approaches may be combined with adopting Focusing attitudes and keeping a certain distance. Counselors can use these approaches until clients regain their ability to be in process. Empathic listening responses are then typically sufficient to allow spiritual experiences to occur.

Six Focusing Steps

Focusing is a process of paying attention to something unclear in one's experience and letting it unfold into new, explicit meanings, understandings, or insights. Although Focusing is a natural, flowing process, the Focusing Method is frequently divided into steps for teaching purposes.

In this chapter the Six Focusing Steps (Gendlin, 1981) are explained. I will present an example of leading a client through a six-step Focusing process that leads to spiritual growth. Practical suggestions to help counselors decide when to use Focusing to integrate spirituality in counseling are given, and various uses of the Focusing Method are described.

Preparation

The Focusing process generally works better when the client or Focuser is somewhat relaxed. Therefore, before beginning the Focusing process, it is often helpful for the client to prepare for Focusing by becoming physically comfortable and relaxed. Noticing one's breathing and one's body in a general way may be used to quiet the mind.

The following instructions may be given to help prepare a client for Focusing:

> Now, you can get comfortable and relaxed and notice your breathing. Notice how your breath goes in and out of your body. Notice how your body is making contact with the chair and how your feet are making contact with the floor.

Additional suggestions for relaxation may be added as needed or requested by a client. For example, if a client is tense, I may give instructions to relax different parts of the body from head to toe.

Some people have trouble Focusing in counseling because they are distracted by a number of problems. These problems, which are mostly in the background, make it difficult to concentrate on one problem or one felt sense. For this reason, it is helpful for clients to set aside their problems temporarily, so that they can choose one problem on which to Focus. This is called Clearing a Space. Also, problems are set aside in order to separate them from each other, to perceive them more clearly, and to feel better physically to work on one of the issues.

Step 1: Clearing a Space

In this step, the client is instructed to take an inventory of currently felt problems or issues. The client checks to see how each issue feels inside, senses the whole vague complexity involved in it, and imagines setting it aside.

Setting aside problems or issues may be done by imagining setting a problem on the floor, putting it in a picture frame, or placing it in a container, such as a box or a trunk. Clients may use whatever image helps them set a problem out temporarily, giving them a better feeling inside. After all the currently felt issues are identified, felt, and set aside, the client chooses one issue to Focus on, usually the problem that is felt most strongly.

The following instructions, given in three parts, may be used for Clearing a Space:

1. In a friendly, gentle way you can ask yourself, "How am I now?" and name something standing in the way of your feeling all O.K. right now. As you name it, notice how the whole thing feels in your body.

When the client has reported the problem and its accompanying feeling, the therapist can say:

2. Then you can imagine setting the whole problem with the feeling aside.

When the client reports that this has been done (and the client often describes how he or she has set the problem aside), the therapist can ask:

3. How would you feel if you didn't have that whole issue?

This last instruction helps the client stay with the feeling that results from setting the problem aside. When the client has described a new feeling, the therapist can return to the first instruction and go through the sequence again with the next problem. This sequence is repeated until the client reports that all the problems have been set aside.

Many clients report that they have spiritual experiences after Clearing a Space. After setting issues out and noticing how it would feel without their problems, clients report feeling less tense and more relaxed, calm, centered, expanded, peaceful, and more able to accept themselves, others, and life.

At times people choose to do only the Clearing a Space step without continuing with the rest of the Focusing steps. I sometimes use this step before seeing a client or doing some task for which I want to be clear-headed. Mental health professionals may wish to use this step for stress reduction and burnout prevention.

Clearing a Space is especially helpful for clients who are overwhelmed by their emotions. On the other hand, if clients are very distant from their feelings, I may omit this step. Clearing a Space may be confusing for such clients and make it even more difficult to identify feelings.

In a counseling session, clients often begin by discussing a chosen issue. If clients are not distracted by other issues, they may be able to Focus on the chosen issue. In this case, the counselor may omit Step 1, Clearing a Space, and begin with Step 2, Getting a Felt Sense.

Step 2: Getting a Felt Sense

In this step, the counselor suggests that the client attend to the whole complex feeling of a problem, the "felt sense." For example, the counselor might ask, "How does this whole thing feel in your bodily now?" or the counselor might suggest, "You could take time to gently sense how that whole issue feels inside now. Welcome it, and notice if you can create a caring, kind atmosphere around it."

At first the felt sense is vague and unclear. It is important to stay with this vague, unclear feeling in a gentle, welcoming way.

Step 3: Finding a Handle

In this step, the client finds words to describe the qualities of the felt sense. Gendlin calls these words a "handle" because they are like the handle of a suitcase. These words help a client hold on to or stay in touch with the vague felt sense or "pull it back" if awareness of it is lost.

The felt sense is multifaceted. It involves emotional qualities and body sensations. It may also involve images, movements, sounds, and smells. Examples of handle words that describe emotional qualities and body sensations are "empty," "jumpy," or "expanding." Examples of images are "shaped like a funnel" or "a river running down my middle." An example of a movement might be "swaying back and forth" or "jumping up and down." A sound might involve "a sharp, piercing sound" or a melody. A smell might be "pungent" or "sweet." I recommend that clients stay with a felt sense until they have found at least several descriptive words. Spending plenty of time with the felt sense usually allows more meaning to come from it later in the process.

To help clients find their handle words, the therapist might say, "You can take time to be with all of that, and notice the words or images that come to describe your feeling."

Step 4: Resonating

In this step, the client checks if the handle words found in Step 3 are the best words to describe the felt sense at the present time. The client may change the words or find additional words to describe the felt sense. At times, resonating may simply involve being with the felt sense.

The following instructions might be used to help a client resonate: "You could check to see if you have just the right words, and notice if there are any other words or symbols to describe the feel of this whole thing." The counselor might also ask the client, "Where in your body do you feel that?"

Step 5: Asking

In this step, the counselor may suggest that the client ask the felt sense an open-ended question, for example, "What is it about this whole issue that leaves you feeling this way?" Asking an open-ended question frequently brings new meanings or answers for the client. Asking such a question is a way of giving the felt sense or the feeling a friendly hearing. The client directs the question to the felt sense and continues to attend to it, waiting for an answer. Usually an answer will emerge in a minute or less, although sometimes an answer will come later. More information about the Asking Step is presented in the next chapter.

When a new felt meaning emerges from the felt sense, the feeling changes, and a "felt shift" occurs. At this point, there is a physiological relief or release. When a felt shift occurs, the client knows that the change is genuine, rather than mere intellectualization. If a client gets an answer, but no felt shift occurs, then the answer is probably only mental. The felt shift indicates that psychospiritual growth has occurred.

Step 6: Receiving

In this step, the counselor helps the client take time to integrate a felt shift. After a client has experienced a felt shift, the counselor needs to affirm it to help the client integrate the many resulting bodily felt changes. For example, the counselor can affirm a felt shift by repeating the words that came with the felt shift and by suggesting that the client take time to notice the bodily felt difference and the new knowing that came with it. The following suggestion may be given to the client: "Take time to savor the new feeling and become familiar with it. You might even ask the new feeling, 'What's the best of this for me?'" The counselor can also affirm the client's felt shift in a nonverbal manner by sitting more upright, by looking more interested, or by putting more excitement into voice tone.

When a felt sense unfolds and a felt shift occurs in Focusing, the client usually changes in many areas and in thousands of respects. The resulting differences are noticeable both in the moments immediately following the felt shift and in later reports from the client.

Gendlin (1964) has referred to the broad way in which the client is changed as *wider application* or *global application*. He said that "the individual is often flooded by many different associations, memories, situations, and circumstances" (pp. 120–121) following a felt shift. For example, clients may say, "Oh, and that's why I feel frozen when someone says this-and-this" or "Oh, and also back when this and this happened, I did the *same* thing." During this period of global application the individual might instead sit in silence and only occasionally voice some of the pieces from this flood.

Example of the Six Focusing Steps

The following example demonstrates how I led a client through a formal, six-step Focusing process and how this process led the client to experience the spiritual dimension. The example has been simplified to demonstrate my use of the Focusing steps.

> Mr. A., a professional football player, came to me for a Focusing session. He told me that he had always been very much in control of his emotions. In the past year there had been a fire in his house, and his 14 year-old son had been arrested for drug use. He said that neither incident had "really fazed" him. However, recently he had gone to his doctor for a check-up, and his blood pressure had been slightly high. He was baffled by the anxiety that resulted. His thinking was going in circles. He kept telling himself that there was nothing to worry about, but his anxiety continued.
>
> I first gave the client Focusing preparation instructions to quiet his mind. I invited him to get comfortable and relaxed and notice his breathing. Then I led him through the first Focusing step, Clearing a Space. I said, "When you are ready you could ask yourself, 'How am I now, and what stands in the way of my feeling all O.K.?'" As he named each issue, I asked him, "How does this whole thing feel in your body now?" As he noticed how the house fire felt in his body, he realized that there was some remaining fear and sadness about the losses involved. After he imagined setting aside this issue, along with the fear and sadness, he felt some relief.
>
> Then as he thought about his son, he noticed his sadness and anger about the arrest. He imagined putting this issue, along with his sadness and anger, into a place where his son was staying. Again he felt some easing. He then named the news from the doctor about his slightly high blood pressure. He said that it felt like a large, prickly ball with anxiety in it.

As he imagined setting this issue, along with the anxiety, outside of himself, he breathed a sigh of relief. I suggested that he stay with the feeling of relief and let me know when he was ready to continue. I then invited the client to set all three issues out in front of him and ask his body which one seemed to need his attention most. He identified the last issue for Focusing.

In Step 2, Getting a Felt Sense, I suggested that he notice again how the "whole thing" concerning the news from the doctor felt in his body.

In Step 3, Finding a Handle, he reported that it still felt like a large prickly ball. He added that it could grow larger than himself and overwhelm him.

In Step 4, Resonating, I suggested that he stay with the feel of the whole thing and notice if he had just the right words or if he had any additional words to describe his feeling. He replied that he had the right words and that he noticed that the ball was also "dark."

In Step 5, Asking, I asked him, "What was it about the news from the doctor that leaves you with a large, prickly, dark ball with anxiety in it?" He directed this question to the felt sense and waited a few moments. With a big sigh of relief he said, "the straw that broke the camel's back." He then realized that he had repressed his emotions about the fire in his house and his son's arrest. He said, "Oh, now I see that this blood pressure thing isn't so important. What's really bothering me is the fire and the kid." He said that he felt relieved and much more relaxed. The client reported that he no longer felt the anxiety.

In Step 6, Receiving, I suggested that he stay with and notice the feelings of relief and relaxation that came with the words *the straw that broke the camel's back*. After the client had taken the time to experience his felt shift, he said that he was able to take his emotions more seriously. In a later session he reported that he was more able to accept the emotions of other people in his life.

It could be said that this example illustrates a spiritual experience because the client paid attention to a subtle, bodily feeling with vague meanings that brought new, clearer meanings involving a transcendent growth process. The subtle, bodily feeling was his felt sense of a large, dark, prickly ball with anxiety in it. The vague meanings were indicated by the word *like*. This word indicated that there was more there than just the feeling. When the felt sense unfolded and the feeling shifted, the new, clearer meaning that came was "the straw that broke the camel's back." The experience involved a transcendent growth process because the client transcended his former frame of reference in that he was able to accept or reach out to more parts of himself, namely the emotional parts of himself. In a later session he reported that the experience helped him accept not only his own emotions but also the emotions of other people.

This example illustrates how Focusing often leads clients to experience their spirituality and consequently undergo psychospiritual growth. Frequent use of the word *whole* during the Focusing process (as in Steps 1, 2, and 4) leads clients to larger structures and larger wholes. This invites clients to go beyond the details of an issue to consider the whole issue, their whole self, their whole relationship, their whole life, the whole human race, the whole planet, and the whole universe. By moving in a direction of higher and broader scope, clients are able to experience a transcendent or spiritual dimension.

Many people would not consider this experience to be spiritual because it does not seem sufficiently dramatic or life-changing. However, the therapist needs to be open to the possibility that the experience might be considered spiritual. If the client perceives the experience to be spiritual, I would agree with the client, given my definition. If the client did not mention the spiritual aspects of this experience, I would not raise the topic.

The Six Focusing Steps in Practice

The counselor needs to decide when to use Focusing with clients. I use Focusing most frequently with clients who are able to identify their emotions and with clients who have either received Focusing training or have a natural ability to Focus. Clients with a natural ability to Focus speak about presently felt nuances of feelings and meanings. Clients who have difficulty identifying emotions typically take longer to learn Focusing. I teach these clients to identify bodily sensations and emotions before teaching them to Focus.

The Focusing Method may be used in at least two ways in counseling: in a complete Focusing round and in "mini-focusings" (Friedman, 1995). A Focusing round consists of guided movement through all or most of the Focusing steps described in this chapter.

"Mini-focusings," on the other hand, consist of one or more Focusing questions or suggestions being used within a session. For example, after a client describes a difficult situation, the counselor might ask (Step 2, Felt Sense), "How does this whole issue feel inside your body now?" At another point the counselor might ask the client (Step 5, Asking), "What's the worst of this whole thing for you?" At any time during the counseling session when needed, the counselor might suggest that the client find more distance or adopt a more friendly attitude.

Focusing-Oriented Psychotherapy (Gendlin, 1996) provides a theoretical framework for the use of Focusing as well as other psychotherapeutic methods used in counseling. The basic rule in Focusing-Oriented Psychotherapy is *Whatever is said or done in psychotherapy must be checked with the felt sense before and after any intervention to see if it brings easing and more life energy.* Checking can be done by asking the client, "How does this whole thing feel in your body now? or "How does this whole thing feel inside now?" before and after an intervention. This rule may be applied to the use of any psychotherapeutic method. When it is applied to the use of Focusing, the misuse of the Focusing Method is almost impossible.

The basic rule of helping clients continually check their felt sense empowers them to trust their inward-originating processes. Clients are encouraged *not* to accept interpretations or suggestions from the therapist that do not fit their inner sense of things.

Conclusion

In this chapter a six-step Focusing teaching method has been described, and an example has been presented. In the next chapter, Asking, Step 5, is discussed in more detail.

To learn to use the Focusing Method in counseling, it is essential to first experience the process yourself. Reading about Focusing can bring about, at best, only a partial understanding of it. I recommend learning Focusing from an experienced Focusing trainer (see Appendix B). Short of this, I suggest reading the Focusing instructions to another person and then having another person read the instructions to you. For this purpose, you will find a set of instructions in Appendix A.

In addition to using the Focusing Method in counseling, it may also be used as a self-help method or in a peer-counseling relationship (Campbell & McMahon, 1985; Cornell, 1990, 1996; Friedman, 1995; Hinterkopf, 1983; Hinterkopf & Brunswick, 1975, 1981; Hinterkopf, Brunswick, & Burbridge, 1975; McGuire, 1981).

CHAPTER

Asking

Asking, Step 5 of the 6 Focusing Steps, is the step in which open-ended questions are asked of the felt sense to allow new meanings to come from it. Focusing questions developed by Gendlin and his associates (Gendlin, 1981) include such questions as, "What is it about this whole thing that feels that way?" "What's the worst about this whole thing for you?" and "What does this whole thing need?" These questions are extremely powerful for facilitating the psychospiritual growth process and for helping clients elicit new meanings from their feelings.

The Asking Step helps facilitate the Focusing process in at least two ways. First, the Asking Step can help clients go further in their Focusing process than if it were omitted. Asking Focusing questions helps clients stay with their process longer and get beyond a block or a sense of being stuck. Furthermore, the Asking Step frequently helps bring about a felt shift that leads to psychospiritual growth. Often the answer that comes is about a different way of being with an issue, a way of being that includes more of oneself, others, and life.

Second, the Asking Step can help keep clients from getting distracted from their Focusing process. When the questions are asked in a friendly, gentle, patient way, they invite clients to stay with a felt sense to see what comes. A Focusing question may keep a client's mind from wandering or going blank while Focusing. (Mind wandering includes both the chattering mind in general and the inner critic in particular.)

In this chapter I describe the Asking Step in more detail. Examples from counseling sessions and guidelines for using the Focusing questions to facilitate the psychospiritual growth process are presented.

Example of Asking

The following example shows how the Focusing question, "What does this whole thing need?" points a client in a transcendent direction. When asking this question, the client asks what the whole thing needs from within or from a source of inner wisdom. The person Focusing allows the answer to come from the felt sense rather than trying to consciously produce the answer or new meanings.

> Ms. B., a 40-year-old female client, had struggled in previous sessions with abandonment issues. Because she was in the hospital for an operation, I did a counseling session by telephone. In addition to feeling physical pain, she was in turmoil because she felt that her husband had abandoned her emotionally, even after she had asked him for emotional support. After we discussed the possibility of couple counseling, I asked her how she felt inside. Ms. B. felt angry, sad, tired, and "wrecked." After exploring the meanings involved in the feelings, she reported still feeling a deep aching. I suggested, "You might try asking, 'What does this whole thing need?'"
>
> She remained with her feeling of deep aching for several moments and then received an image of something in her stomach cradling the part that had been operated on. She felt an energy in the form of a guardian angel holding the "injured me." In her image, a path connected her to a broad horizon. With marked relief (at the time of her felt shift) she said, "I don't feel so alone anymore." She felt light, and the pain was gone. She reported that this was the first time she had experienced her spirituality. The client said she realized that this "spiritual part" could nurture her emotionally even when her husband could not. Subsequently, the client experienced more autonomy in various areas of her life.

Asking the Focusing question "What does this whole thing need?" helped bring new, explicit meanings. These new, explicit meanings included the client not "feeling so alone anymore" and realizing that the "spiritual part" could nurture her even when her husband could not.

About the Asking Step

Some of the following information about Asking is detailed and advanced. You may wish to experience Focusing before reading this information. If you are unable to experience Focusing with a Focusing trainer, you might try having someone who knows reflective listening read the Focusing Instructions to you. These instructions can be found in Appendix A.

The Focusing questions need to be asked in a gentle, friendly, patient way to encourage the client to take a similar attitude toward his or her own felt sense. Frequently, questions are asked in a tentative way and embedded in suggestions to make them sound more gentle. For example, a counselor might start a question by saying, "You could ask yourself," or "You might try asking." The counselor would then state the question as follows: "You might try asking, 'What's the worst of this whole thing for me?'" The question is also embedded in a suggestion so that the client can easily disregard the question or ask for a different question. This empowers clients to be in charge of their own process.

Clients need to ask Focusing questions of the felt sense, rather than simply trying to figure out an answer to a question mentally. Words or images that come from the felt sense usually come more slowly than words that are used to answer questions mentally. Words that come from the felt sense usually arise only a few at a time with frequent pauses between words. Usually the words do not sound intellectualized and do not come in complete sentences. The words that come from the felt sense frequently bring an element of surprise. The client may feel puzzled by them at first. These words or images match the body feelings and usually bring at least a small sense of relief or release in the body. If a client seems to answer a question in a mental way, the counselor may invite the client to check the answer with the felt sense to see if it brings easing. If the client says that the answer has not brought easing, I usually suggest that he or she ask a slightly different question of the same type.

For instance, suppose that I have asked the client, "What does this whole thing need?" and the client has given me a mental-sounding answer such as, "It must be that it needs forgiveness." I would then say, "You could check that answer with your body to see if it brought easing." If the client says that it did not bring easing, I might try asking a slightly different question such as, "How would this whole thing feel if it were all O.K.?"

A few clients prefer to omit the Asking Step because it results in their feeling too pressured to produce an answer. They prefer only an invitation, stated as a suggestion, such as, "You can be with all of that in a friendly, gentle way and see what comes." I offer this alternative to clients and frequently give this suggestion after asking an open-ended Focusing question. I also suggest that clients tell me at any time during the process which suggestion they would like me to give.

The Focusing questions in Step 5 usually start with the word *what* instead of *why*. "Why" questions, such as "Why do you feel that way?" may lead clients away from their experiencing to intellectualizing about reasons for their problems. In contrast, "what" questions help clients stay with their present feelings.

The Focusing questions in Step 5 are open-ended instead of closed-ended. Closed-ended questions may be answered with "yes," "no," or a few words. An example of a closed-ended question is, "Do you think that your relationship with your parents may have contributed to this problem?" The Focusing questions are open-ended to help clients stay with their process and to allow maximum room for exploration.

After the client answers an open-ended "what" question, it is important that the counselor check back with a client's felt sense to see if the felt sense affirms the answer. If the felt sense affirms the answer, the client will experience a sense of rightness and some degree of easing. Steps 2 through 5 are usually recycled until the client experiences a felt shift or a more profound release.

The following example includes Focusing instructions I might use to help a client recycle Steps 2 and 5, using a different question in Step 5 each time. For this illustration I have omitted Steps 3 and 4 (Finding a Handle and Resonating) to emphasize the recycling of Steps 2 and 5.

- What is it about this whole thing that leaves you feeling this way? (Step 5)

- How does this whole thing feel in your body now? (Step 2)
- What's the worst of this whole thing for you? (Step 5)
- How does this whole thing feel in your body now? (Step 2)
- What does this whole thing need right now? (Step 5)
- How does this whole thing feel in your body now? (Step 2)

On rare occasions, it is time to end a session even though a felt shift has not occurred. I then suggest that the client promise the uncomfortable feeling that he or she will come back to it. Of course, at the beginning of the next session the client will need to begin with whatever feelings are most present.

Types of Questions

There are many different Focusing questions that can be asked in Step 5. However, I have found it useful to group them into three types: (a) general questions, (b) crux questions, and (c) felt shift questions (Hinterkopf, 1984).

General questions are asked to learn what the felt sense is about or to help learn what aspect of a problem leads to the client's discomfort. Examples of general questions include the following:

- What is that whole feeling about?
- What is it about this whole thing that feels like this?
- If this whole feeling could talk, what would it say?
- What in your life feels like this?
- What stands in the way of your doing (or believing) that?

Crux questions are asked to narrow the focus, to learn what the heart of a problem is. These questions often help clients go deeper into their experiencing process. Crux questions frequently help me get to the bottom of things sooner with my clients. Examples of crux questions include the following:

- What's the worst of this whole thing for you? (asked of an uncomfortable feeling)
- What's the best of this whole thing for you? (asked of a pleasant feeling)
- What's the crux of this whole thing for you?

- What's the (handle)-est (for example, what's the heaviest) about this whole thing?
- What's most meaningful or most exciting about this whole thing? (asked of something with obvious positive aspects)

Felt shift questions are asked to help the felt sense unfold in a felt shift direction. Of course, a felt shift cannot be produced or controlled. A person can only put himself or herself in the best state of readiness to receive a felt shift. Campbell and McMahon (1985) have referred to the felt shift as "grace." Examples of felt shift questions include the following:

- What does this whole thing need right now?
- What would bring easing?
- How would this whole thing feel if it were all O.K.?

The felt shift question "How would this whole thing feel if it were all O.K.?" is asked to help clients imagine how it would feel if they felt all O.K. about an issue. If clients are able to feel this "all O.K. feeling," they are more likely to get the answers that will help them resolve an issue. During the Focusing process, a felt shift may arise spontaneously without asking a felt shift question. In this case, felt shift questions may be omitted.

Choosing the Type of Question

When facilitating a client's Focusing process, counselors need to decide which type of question (general, crux, or felt shift) would be most effective. I have developed a set of guidelines for this purpose (Hinterkopf, 1984).

I usually start the Asking Step by asking a general question. Then (after having a client check his or her felt sense) I usually ask a crux question. However, if clients have already Focused a little on their own and know what the feeling is about, I might start by asking a crux question. Also, if clients seem confused or too diffuse, I might start with a crux question.

Felt shift questions are more commonly asked near the end of a session after many rounds of Focusing (Getting a Felt Sense, Finding a Handle, Resonating, Asking) have been done to explore an issue.

When a new feeling arises, and clients have had the time to find just the right words (Finding a Handle and Resonating) to describe the new feeling, I suggest that they ask their felt sense a general question again to learn what the new feeling is about.

I have discovered that it is usually most effective when asking Focusing questions to observe the following pattern:

1. *If the Felt Sense stays the same, change the type of question.* Start with a general question. If in response to the general question the felt sense stays the same, change to a crux or felt shift question.
2. *If the Felt Sense Changes, ask the same type of question.* Start with a general question. If in response to the general question the felt sense changes but no felt shift occurs, ask another general question.

The following two examples show this general pattern. The examples have been simplified; for instance, listening responses, pauses, and Steps 3 and 4 (Finding a Handle and Resonating) have been deleted to highlight the asking patterns.

1. *If the Felt Sense stays the same, change the type of question.*

C: I have this feeling of *tightness* in my stomach.
T: What is that whole feeling of tightness about? (General question)
C: The relationship with my husband.
T: How does this whole thing feel in your body now?
C: It still feels *tight*.
T: What's the worst of this whole thing for you? (Crux question)
C: The worst is that we can't talk with each other.
T: How does this whole thing feel in your body now?
C: It feels less tight, but it still feels somewhat *tight*.
T: Perhaps you could try asking, "What does this whole thing need?" (Felt Shift question)
C: Answers with easing in her face and body, "I need to learn to listen to myself more."
T: How does it feel in your body now?
C: More relaxed and strong.

2. If the Felt Sense changes, ask the same type of question.

C: I have this feeling of *tightness* in my stomach.
T: What in your life leaves you with that feeling of tightness in your stomach? (General question)

C: The relationship with my husband.

T: How does this whole thing feel in your body now?

C: It feels *sad and heavy.*

T: What is it about this whole issue that feels sad and heavy?"
(General question)

This asking pattern has exceptions. The overriding rule is that the therapist using Focusing follow the *client's* process. As clients learn more about Focusing, they learn to ask themselves the questions they need for moving their process forward. As clients learn more self-guiding, counselors can ask fewer questions.

Conclusion

Because the questions used in the Asking Step are powerful in facilitating the psychospiritual growth process, I have devoted an entire chapter to this step. Counselors first trying to use these questions may be tempted to use other questions, such as closed questions and "why" questions. If other questions are attempted, I invite the counselor to carefully observe the client's verbal and nonverbal responses and compare them to the client's responses when Focusing questions are asked. At times, I continue to be astonished by the degree to which the Focusing questions lead the client deeper into process and other questions lead the client away from process.

CHAPTER

Working With Spiritual Process

K nowing the difference between spiritual content and spiritual process is important for learning to facilitate spiritual growth in counseling. *Spiritual content* refers to symbolized material with meaning idiosyncratic to each client, such as God, Allah, Mother Earth, Kundalini, and past life. In contrast, *spiritual process* involves paying attention to a wholistic, bodily feeling (a felt sense) in a special way that allows the unfolding of greater easing and life energy. In this process, more explicit meanings that involve the transcendent dimension emerge.

If counselors pay attention only to spiritual content, they may miss opportunities to facilitate important spiritual growth. For example, when a counselor is uninformed about a particular type of spiritual content, he or she may be tempted to ignore it or judge it. In either case, the counselor might fail to respond in a way that facilitates the client's process. On the other hand, if the counselor attends to spiritual process, then he or she can respond to the client in a way that facilitates spiritual growth. This can be done by reflecting a client's felt sense words, asking Focusing questions, and at times making Focusing suggestions such as reminding a client to keep the Focusing attitudes.

Following the client's experiencing process by learning Focusing is also an effective way for a therapist to develop a more open attitude. It is important for counselors to be able to work with clients having a wide variety of viewpoints about spirituality. Through the

experience of facilitating the Focusing process in others, the therapist learns that material that is at first difficult to understand may
be valuable for the psychospiritual growth process.

In this chapter the following guidelines for facilitating a client's
psychospiritual process using Focusing are provided: (a) following
experiencing process rather than content, (b) Focusing on spiritual experiences that begin with positive feelings, (c) Focusing on
spiritual experiences that begin with uncomfortable feelings, and
(d) Focusing on blocks to spiritual experiences. Examples in this
chapter illustrate how to help clients work through a variety of
spiritual issues, including those involving spiritual emergency and
spiritual repression.

Following Experiencing Process Rather Than Content

The Focusing Method can be used to work with clients whose
spiritual experiences have content different from that found in the
counselor's own spiritual experiences. For example, even though I
have not had a past life experience[1], I have used Focusing effec-
tively to help clients work with such experiences. In the next example, the Focusing question, "What in your life feels like this?"
helps ground the client and helps him relate his past life experience to a present life issue.

> Mr. G. was overwhelmed by a past life experience. He told me
> about an experience in which he was a female Egyptian slave
> who had been chained and beaten. He was dragged along a
> dirt road and thrown in a jail to rot and die. He still carried
> the pain of this experience in his body. I asked him how this
> whole thing felt in his body now. He said that he felt pain in
> his muscles and bones. His flesh felt bruised and torn. I asked
> him, "What is the worst of this whole thing for you?" After a

---

[1] Belief in past life experiences generally relates to one's culture. For example, a belief in reincarnatioin is typically found in Buddhist and Hindu
religions. However, past life experiences, such as Mr. G.'s experience, can
occur in Western culture even though the predominant Judeo-Christian religion is not receptive to them. Like many other psychotherapists, I have
found that working with past life content material has been useful to the
therapeutic process of the clients who have had these experiences.

long pause of almost 30 seconds, he said that the worst of it was that he felt so helpless. He reported still feeling pain.

I asked him what in his present life felt like this. His attention returned to his felt sense for some time. Then he said that his work situation felt like this. After exploring this issue I asked him what the whole thing needed. He paused several moments and said with visible relief that it needed for him to break free and leave the situation. The client told me that the pain was gone and that he felt more relaxed and had more energy. In the next counseling session Mr. G. reported that he had been more assertive at work.

This example illustrates a spiritual process because the client was more able to accept and embrace the assertive parts of himself. As he transcended his former frame of reference (of feeling helpless and being less assertive), he felt more easing and life energy.

The example also shows how Focusing can help ground clients experiencing spiritual emergency. These clients may be given a diagnosis of *DSM-IV* Code V62.89 Religious or Spiritual Problem (American Psychiatric Association, 1994). Spiritual emergency involves spiritual content accompanied by distressing feelings because the content, in this case the client's past life experience, cannot be readily integrated into the personality (Chandler, Holden, & Kolander, 1992). Grounding is experienced when clients become more aware of bodily feelings, and integration of spiritual content occurs as extraordinary material is connected to current life issues.

Focusing on Spiritual Experiences That Begin With Positive Feelings

When clients mention positive aspects of their religion or spirituality, I usually help them explore these aspects experientially. Exploring these positive aspects can help them develop personal strength and autonomy, strengthen the positive effects of counseling, and make their religious faith more of an experiential reality.

When Focusing on spiritual experiences that begin with positive feelings, I find the following Focusing questions especially helpful: "What's best about this whole thing for you?" "What feels the most meaningful in this whole thing for you?" and

"What feels most important about this whole thing for you?" These questions help the client expand, deepen, and differentiate spiritual experiences that already exist.

> Ms. T. mentioned in a counseling session that her Christian faith was important to her. I invited her to explore the experience of her faith more deeply by asking her, "What's most important to you about your faith?" After directing her attention inside, she responded that being part of a larger plan gave her a better perspective on things. I asked her, "How does knowing that feel inside right now?" She paused and answered, "It feels smooth and clear." I encouraged her to stay with that feeling. After a time I suggested that she might ask herself, "What's best about this for me?" After a long pause she replied, "that I can set aside the tension from all that worrying that I do." She then reported feeling "smooth and clear and very peaceful." In the next session she reported being more able to accept things that could not be changed.

This example illustrates how positive spiritual experiences can be opportunities for spiritual growth. In addition to responding sensitively to the client, the counselor can facilitate new life-giving experiences involving the spiritual dimension by responding to spiritual process.

Notice how the same types of questions may be used with a person from a different religious background to help deepen and expand his religious experience. Even though the spiritual content is different, the spiritual process of Mr. S. is similar to Ms. T.'s process in the previous example.

> Mr. S., from a Hindu religious background, said that "Vishnu, the protector of people, who holds a wheel in his hand," was very important to him. I asked him, "How does that symbol or image feel?" After several moments of paying attention inside he said, "It feels peaceful, and I'm surrounded by a glow around me, like a mother's embrace."
>
> I then asked him, "What's the best of that for you?" After a pause he reported, "It's always there for me. Vishnu is embodied in many forms, animate and inanimate, male and female. This gives me peace of mind. For example, in one form he might give me advice or in another form comfort. Vishnu can also be seen in the changing seasons. I can always talk with Vishnu. Now in the autumn I feel the presence of Vishnu.

It gives me courage for my work and school." I then asked him, "How does the image of Vishnu feel in your body now?" He replied, "I feel hope and I feel invigorated all over, especially in my arms, like I'm ready to face a challenge, more confident."

Focusing on Spiritual Experiences That Begin With Uncomfortable Feelings

Spiritual experience is not limited to only positive feelings. It often begins with feelings of vague discomfort or even painful feelings, such as sadness, anger, fear, or confusion. Although a spiritual experience may begin with uncomfortable feelings, it eventually involves a felt shift or a presently felt experience of easing and more life energy. If clients have spiritual issues that involve distressing feelings, it is important to encourage them to Focus on these feelings to explore them.

Ms. F. was experiencing a spiritual "desert." Her spiritual life was feeling "blah." I asked her how her spiritual life was feeling in her body. She said it felt very neutral and empty, as if everything were the same. She had an image of an Arab sitting next to a camel in a desert. She said that this was a good image for her current spiritual life. I suggested that she ask inside, "What does this whole thing need right now?" She reported that the Arab stood up slowly and led the camel across the desert. Ms. F. said, "I don't know how he knows which direction to go in." Then, as she realized that the Arab was following his intuition, she knew that she had to do this more in her spiritual life, too. When I asked her how this whole thing felt in her body now, she reported that it felt alive and peaceful.

Ms. F. was able to transcend her more limited former frame of reference in which she placed an overemphasis on thinking to the exclusion of intuition. Even though her experience began with uncomfortable feelings regarding her spiritual life, it presented an opportunity for spiritual growth. Counselors need not stop at empathizing with such uncomfortable feelings (although such empathy is necessary for the process), but can use the Focusing Method to facilitate further positive change.

Although several of the previous examples have indicated that clients needed to be more in touch with feelings and intuition, there are an unlimited number of other possibilities for what may be needed in a client's life. In the next example of Focusing on a spiritual experience that begins with an uncomfortable feeling, the client realizes that he needs to learn to think more clearly.

> Mr. P., a client with a history of alcoholism and drug abuse, was recovering from a painfully chaotic life. He had an image of himself in a dark, chaotic jungle. His felt sense was painful, confused, and jumbled. When he asked himself what the whole thing needed, he received an image that brought easing and a feeling of breathing in clear air. In the new image he saw some Greek pillars at a short distance. He was able to hold on to the Greek pillars and pull himself out of the jungle. He then realized that the Greek pillars represented clear thinking and that he needed more of this in his life. In subsequent sessions we concentrated on cognitive work.

Focusing on Blocks to Spiritual Experiences

Some clients have had abusive religious experiences that turn them away from exploring positive, growth-producing aspects of their religion. Such negative religious experiences can result in an inability to experience religious content or subject matter in a positive way.

It is generally believed that people become more integrated and whole by exploring their roots. This is especially true of exploring one's religious and spiritual roots, because these religious and spiritual symbols carry so many important implicit meanings. Therefore, even when a religion practiced during a client's childhood seems more abusive than growth producing, I still encourage the client to Focus on these uncomfortable and sometimes painful feelings. Usually clients who Focus on these negative religious experiences over time eventually experience and integrate those parts of the religion that are more positive.

> In a workshop, Ms. C. said that she presently had negative feelings about God. She thought that this "block" kept her from experiencing her spirituality. Ms. C., who was raised and

confirmed in the Lutheran church in East Germany, said that she had positive experiences of God in her childhood. She married a man who emotionally and physically abused her, but her church and her family admonished her to stay with him. From that time on the client felt "a hole of pain" in her stomach that felt like "a deep wound with a scar over it." She saw God as someone who wanted her to suffer as a victim of her husband. After many years she broke away from her husband and in the process also broke away from God and the church.

Ms. C. said that she would like to Focus on the deep wound in her stomach and her hatred toward God. As she continued to be with these feelings, she felt anger at God crawl through her whole body. The worst of it was that she had "a hard pipe inside" to protect her, but the pipe also separated her from God and from other people. After exploring her feelings for some time, the client asked what the whole thing needed. She received the answer that it needed "permission to be reunited with a God that didn't demand senseless suffering." The client was then able to feel protection and a relaxed, warm love from God. She reported that the session had opened her to and reunited her with an important part of herself that lay in the shadows. By reconnecting with her repressed, positive, childhood experience of God, she was able to feel more whole.

This example illustrates how the Focusing Method can be used to help clients work through religious problems (in this case the block was religious abuse). Ms. C. was able to reconnect with her positive childhood spiritual experience of God and find new spiritual experiences of feeling protection and a relaxed, warm love from God and feeling more whole.

Conclusion

Spiritual problems may take the form of spiritual emergency (as with Mr. G.'s overwhelming past life experience) or repression of spiritual experiences (as with Ms. C.'s positive experience of God). The Focusing Method may be used to help ground clients experiencing spiritual emergency and to help open clients to repressed spiritual content (often experienced as blocks). Because the Focusing Method helps clients identify and connect physical-emotional feelings with meanings, clients are able to reexperience a sense of emotional balance. This frequently opens the way to spiritual development.

CHAPTER

Special Considerations Regarding Content

W hat has been said so far has mostly referred to applying the Focusing Method to facilitate a client's psychospiritual process. I will now discuss some special considerations regarding spiritual content. Content refers to symbolized material with meaning idiosyncratic to each client, such as God, Allah, Mother Earth, or past life or near-death experiences. Because spiritual content frequently carries such rich and powerful meanings, counselors need to respond sensitively to the client's spiritual material.

In this chapter I address special issues regarding content traditionally considered spiritual. These issues include the following: (a) learning about the client's religious tradition and spiritual orientation, (b) using the client's words, (c) asking spiritually oriented Focusing questions, and (d) recognizing contraindications for using spiritually oriented Focusing questions.

Learning About the Client's Religious Tradition or Spiritual Orientation

I begin learning about the client's religious tradition or spiritual orientation in the initial intake interview. Questions I ask include, "Do you have a religious preference or spiritual orientation?" and "What religion was practiced in your home when you were a child?"

If a client talks about not being religious, but being a spiritual person, I might ask, "How do you experience your spirituality?" What I learn from the client's answers to these questions will help me facilitate his or her spiritual process in the course of counseling. Also, asking these questions in the intake interview suggests that the subject of spirituality, which includes religion, is an acceptable and relevant dimension of counseling (Kelly, 1995).

Using the Client's Words

Because words have special meanings or connotations for each person, the counselor needs to be careful to use the same words as the client when working with spiritual issues. For example, if the client uses the theistic term *God*, it is usually most helpful for the therapist to use the same word when responding to the client. I learn the client's vocabulary from the questions I ask in the intake interview and in subsequent counseling sessions.

The following two examples illustrate the need for a counselor to be comfortable with using both theistic and nontheistic terms. In the first example the client uses theistic words such as *God* and *Jesus Christ*. In the second example the client is not able to relate his experience to theistic words but is able to respond to the question, "What is your experience of being related to something greater than yourself?" In both cases I tried to use the client's words because I thought they would help lead the client to experience more easing and life energy and consequently spiritual growth.

Example of Using Theistic Terms

After months of work on issues arising from the religion practiced during her childhood, Ms. L. said, "I wish I could feel something positive about Jesus Christ, but I have all these negative feelings, including a lot of tension and anger." When I asked her what all that tension and anger was about, the answer that came was "separation"—the way her relatives had used Jesus Christ to separate themselves from other people. Then I asked her, "If that whole separation issue weren't there, what would your feelings about Jesus Christ be?" She answered, "Then I would feel forgiveness with feelings of warmth and acceptance." The client was then able to experience these feelings in relationship to Jesus Christ.

Example of Using Nontheistic Terms

Mr. K. said that he was spiritual but had difficulty relating to the term *God*. After discussing the issue involved, I asked him, "What is your experience of being related to something greater than yourself?" The client said, "It feels like getting in touch with a larger background where you're aware of feeling connected to everyone and everything else." Then I asked him, "How does getting in touch with a larger background feel in your body right now?" He said, "It feels more relaxed. My body feels bigger and there is a quiet energy. My head feels clearer." When the client said, "I think I just had a spiritual experience," I agreed. Had I insisted on using the term *God*, instead of affirming the client's words, I would have run the risk of hindering or negating the client's spiritual process.

During the counseling process, spiritual content unfamiliar to the counselor may arise unexpectedly. At such times it is especially important that the counselor use the client's terms. In supervising counselors I have sometimes heard counselors tell clients that they cannot relate to the client's experience because it is unfamiliar to them. This unfortunate and unnecessary response usually stops the client's psycho-spiritual process and leaves the client feeling isolated.

The next example illustrates spiritual content that arises unexpectedly in the counseling session. In a multicultural society counselors need to be comfortable with material from any spiritual tradition.

Example of Spiritual Content Arising Unexpectedly

A Chinese woman from a Buddhist background talked about feeling "very tired much of the time." At first she thought it was a physical tiredness from her busy schedule and not enough sleep. But then she realized that her tiredness was due to "too many reincarnations without enough enlightenment." I reflected, "So you feel tired due to too many reincarnations without enough enlightenment." She said, "Life is getting old for me." She explained that she knew that she wasn't here to just live this life but that she was here to get enlightened. Again I responded empathically and reflected her felt sense words.

I then suggested the question, "Perhaps you could ask yourself, 'What does this whole thing need?'" After spending some time with her attention directed inside, she received the answer, "Light and love in the heart area." She realized that she was so tired because she wanted to achieve enlightenment by herself. She said, "Instead I now realize that I need to *receive* enlightenment—that enlightenment is a gift, a moment of grace when I remember to receive light and love from the universe. This is the only way to receive enlightenment." With this answer her tiredness disappeared. I suggested that she stay with her new feeling of easing.

This example also illustrates how the first problem that a client raises is frequently not the issue that is causing the discomfort. In this case, immediately working on a solution to alleviate the client's tiredness could have distracted the client's attention away from a process that led to psychospiritual growth. Instead, by first listening to and guiding a client in Focusing, the counselor can often help a client identify and even resolve the underlying issue. After Focusing, practical solutions to a problem may still be discussed.

Asking Spiritually Oriented Focusing Questions

To help clients experience the transcendent dimension, I have developed a number of questions that I call "spiritually oriented Focusing questions" (Hinterkopf, 1990a). These questions make reference to spiritual content. They include such questions as "How does your relationship with God (or Allah, Christ, Higher Power, or Mother Earth) feel in your body?" "How do you experience God in all this?" and "What is your experience of something greater than yourself in all of this?" These questions can be used in addition to the basic Focusing questions, of "What in your life feels like this?" "What's the worst of this for you?" and "What does this whole thing need?"

Normally, spiritually oriented Focusing questions are used only when clients have previously indicated interest and belief in the transcendent dimension. Clients may have indicated such a belief in the initial intake interview or during a subsequent counseling session.

Usually, spiritually oriented Focusing questions are used near the end of a session after a client has had time to explore uncomfortable feelings. These questions frequently help facilitate a felt shift and psychospiritual growth.

If I know from previous statements that clients have religious or spiritual convictions, I might ask a spiritually oriented Focusing question if they have had a particularly difficult time grappling with a problem. For example, I might ask them, "How do you experience God in all of this?" or "How do you experience something greater than yourself in all of this?" In the following example, asking the client about her experience of God near the end of the session helps bring about a more complete felt shift.

Example of Using a Spiritually Oriented Focusing Question

Ms. N., a single mother familiar with Focusing, was having a conflict with her daughter. The mother reported, "My daughter won't reach out to me after we've had an argument. When I reach out to her, my daughter sarcastically puts me down." After the mother explored her feelings of vulnerability and anger, I asked her, "What does this whole thing need?" She said, "It needs a balance of waiting and reaching out." The mother had hesitation in her voice and said she could tell that the felt shift was not complete.

Because the mother had previously told me that she had a deep faith in God, I asked her, "How do you experience God in all of this?" She waited a few moments and then with a deep sigh of relief said, "I don't have to come up with the answer to all of this myself. There is something larger than both of us that will guide us to find the right answers." Ms. N. reported that she now felt completely at peace.

In the next example I ask a spiritually oriented Focusing question of someone who had previously said that he had no belief in God. On rare occasions, for example at times of crisis, I may raise the subject of a transcendent being, power, or reality when the client has not done so. The death of a loved one, or the imminence of one's own death, might be such an occasion. At such times clients often are more open to the transcendent dimension and find such questions helpful.

Example of Asking a Spiritually Oriented Focusing Question at a Time of Crisis

Mr. W. had left the religion practiced during his childhood. He was now grappling with the recent death of his father, a fundamentalist Christian minister. I asked him how the death of his father felt in his body. He reported that it felt sad and heavy. There were good memories of doing things with his father, such as building things together. Now he grieved this loss.

After giving him time to let tears come, I asked him what the tears were about. In a sad tone of voice he responded, "I have to do it all myself now." When I asked him what this whole thing needed, he said, "I could get a little help from my therapist." I asked him how that felt in his body. He said, "I feel weighted down and tense." (It was obvious that the answer was not helpful at that moment because it did not bring easing.)

From my own experience I know that persons raised in religions that permeate their lives usually have some positive associations with their faith. So, I asked him, "What is your experience of feeling related to something greater than yourself in all this?" I was careful to add, "If you don't connect to that question, feel free to drop it." After waiting a few moments, there was an obvious relaxation with more energy. He said, "Wow! I guess that's what one might call God! I have felt disconnected from that for so many years. That just opened a big new space for me. I don't feel so alone any more."

Contraindications for Using Spiritually Oriented Focusing Questions

When I suggest spiritually oriented Focusing questions to clients, I carefully check if the question brings easing or more life-forward energy. If a question leads a client away from feeling process, I discontinue using the question. For example, if a question resulted in a client experiencing more tension or confusion, I might suggest that the client disregard the question.

When a spiritually oriented Focusing question leads a client away from feeling process during a session in which a felt shift was previously experienced, I try to help the client return to the last point in the session where there was easing.

Example of a Contraindication

Mr. T., who had a doctorate degree in theology, was in the process of divorce and struggling with painful feelings. After exploring these feelings for almost an hour, I asked him, "What does this whole thing need right now?" The answer he received was "I need to spend some time alone." He reported that he felt more calm and relaxed. Because I thought that he only had a partial felt shift, I asked him, "How do you experience God in all this?" After several moments he said, "That question feels really confusing to me. I get into all these arguments in my head."

Because I could see that the spiritually oriented Focusing question led him away from his bodily felt process and into his "head," I suggested, "Perhaps you could go back to that place where you said, 'I need to spend some time alone,' and you felt more calm and relaxed." The client was able to experience the feeling of being more calm and relaxed again.

Usually, spiritually oriented Focusing questions should only be used after the client has had ample time to explore an issue using the basic Focusing questions. A spiritually oriented Focusing question should almost never be used only because the therapist needs to bring the session to a close because of time constraints. Using such a question to bring a session to a close usually results in misuse of the question. If a therapist needs to bring a session to a close and no felt shift has occurred, it is better to help the client "mark" the last felt place. For example, the therapist might gently say, "Perhaps you could promise that heavy feeling about this issue that you will come back to it another time."

Some clients have difficulty relating to questions such as "What is your experience of God in this?" or "How does your relationship with God feel in your body?" They report that these questions are too confusing and open-ended. These people often find it more helpful to think of an attribute of God and then ask how that attribute feels inside.

Example of Thinking of an Attribute and Then Focusing

Ms. B. told me that her religion was important to her but that she had trouble experiencing it. When I asked her, "What is your experience of God in your body," she replied, "I don't feel anything." When I asked her, "What attributes or qualities are associated with God for you?," she said, "love and acceptance." Then I asked her how God's love and acceptance felt in her body. She responded that it felt warm all over—like a bright, sunny day.

Of course, if clients are nonreligious or do not consider themselves to be spiritual, I very rarely use spiritually oriented Focusing questions with them. For example, in the intake interview clients might say, "I'm not religious," "I'm an atheist," "I don't believe in that spiritual stuff," "I would rather not look at that now because I have so many negative feelings connected with it," or "I know I have to deal with that part of my life some time, but now is not the time to do it."

However, if they have a spontaneous spiritual experience in counseling, I might then explain my broader, process definition of spirituality. This provides them with a vocabulary they might find useful for thinking about their experience and for discussing it with other people. For example, if nonreligious clients have experiences of feeling at one with humankind or nature, I might say that I considered their experience to be spiritual because it helped them feel connected to more parts of themselves, others, and life. Clients usually respond positively when I share a process definition of spirituality with them.

Conclusion

In this chapter special issues regarding spiritual content have been addressed and examples have been provided. One area of content I have not addressed is the spiritual symbolization found in dreams. The Focusing Method can be used to work with dreams, including spiritual symbols found in them. Using Focusing with dreams helps people integrate more parts of themselves, others, and life, resulting in more wholeness and spiritual growth. To learn more about this powerful method to work with dreams, refer to Eugene Gendlin's book, *Let Your Body Interpret Your Dreams* (1986).

11

An Excerpt From a Psychotherapy Session

The excerpt in this chapter presents a Focusing part of a psychotherapy session. A Focusing part of a counseling session is the time during which the client is paying attention to vague, implicit feelings and letting them unfold into new, more explicit meanings. This part of a session may last from 5 to 40 minutes. I share the following longer excerpt with you to demonstrate the use of several rounds of Focusing. After the excerpt, some concluding comments are offered.

The client in this excerpt has previously learned Focusing, and we have already established a relationship. She is able to follow my Focusing guiding easily. Examples of working with clients who have more difficulty with Focusing have been presented in previous chapters.

In this excerpt, notice the progression of steps and how they come from within the client. I do not suggest any content solutions. Notice how I follow and facilitate process by asking open-ended Focusing questions, making Focusing suggestions regarding attitude and distance, and giving "exact, empathic listening responses." Exact, empathic listening responses involve saying back feelings and meanings using the same felt sense words as those of the client.

At first, some counselors may think that using the client's exact felt sense words during reflection seems parrot-like and superficial. The deeper the client is in internal process, however, the more important it is to use the client's exact words. When a person is Focusing, the words he or she uses are usually the best possible words. Paraphrasing the client's felt sense words can be counter-productive because it usually brings the client out of bodily process to evaluate whether the paraphrased words exactly match his or her experience. Also, when counselors experience Focusing themselves, they realize how the reflection of exact words helps them go deeper into internal process. This type of reflection requires that the counselor, at least during the Focusing process, trust that a client has inner wisdom or a still, small voice. To use the Focusing Method, it is helpful for a counselor to believe that clients have a natural healing process that seeks wholeness, connectedness, and spiritual growth.

During Focusing, many clients are able to allow their natural healing process to take place when the therapist gives only empathic listening and Focusing responses. Sharing my thoughts with the client during the process might interrupt the process, and the client might have difficulty returning to it. For this reason, if I have any thoughts about the client's content, such as suggestions or interpretations, I might make note of them, but I do not usually share these ideas with the client during the Focusing process. If they still seem relevant, these ideas can be shared with the client *after* the Focusing process and the discussion about it. Similarly, I do not usually introduce other kinds of therapeutic interventions during the Focusing part of a counseling session.

When using Focusing in a therapy session, the therapist may not need to use all six steps. In this excerpt I do not use the Clearing a Space Step because the client's attention is already well focused on one issue. Also, I rarely use Step 4, Resonating, because the client already has many unique descriptive, "handle" words for her felt sense.

When I guide a client in Focusing, I need to slow my own pace to match that of the client. For this reason, when I suggest that the client get comfortable and relaxed in T2, I become somewhat comfortable and relaxed along with the client. During this preparation time, I set out my own thoughts and concerns (as in the Clearing a Space Step in Focusing) to become fully present for the client.

Notice how I remind the client to keep a friendly, gentle Focusing attitude in T5 and how I encourage her to set her whole issue out at a certain distance in T12. This illustrates how something new is allowed to emerge when the client is able to tolerate holding both feelings and both sides of a conflict at the same time. She is then able to feel and see the conflict as a whole.

Near the end of this session in T40 I ask the client a spiritually oriented Focusing question. I use the word God in the question because she had previously told me that her faith in God is very important for her. Although the client has already had a felt shift by this time, I ask a spiritually oriented Focusing question to help her stay with the felt shift longer and help carry her felt shift further.

C1: I have this sad feeling I'd like to look at today. I don't really know what it's about.

The client has a vague, implicit feeling without knowing the explicit meaning. Her saying that she doesn't know what it's about indicates that she senses the presence of some vague, whole thing that is implicit.

T1: Mmhm. So do you want to just check in and see what's there?

I check whether the client would like to do some Focusing. I had previously told her that she could reject this invitation at any time.

C2: Yeah. I think that would be best.

T2: O.K., so you can get comfortable and relaxed and notice your breathing. (Client closes eyes; silence 35 seconds) And then as you let your awareness down into your body, you can ask yourself in a friendly, gentle way, "How am I now, and what's standing in the way of my feeling all O. K.?"

I give the client some preparation instructions. She is able to relax easily. Otherwise I would have given more extensive relaxation instructions.

C3: (Silence, 25 seconds) Well, I notice some mind chatter going on, talking at the back of my head, like.

The client already has an observer self that can notice that her mind is chattering.

T3: So, there's that mind chatter back there.

This is a simple reflection to let her know that I am following her.

C4: And also I notice some sadness like—on-the-verge-of-crying sad. (She cries silently and wipes her tears.)

She notices more than a single emotion of sadness. She notices a larger feeling, a felt sense, an "on-the-verge-of-crying sad." Her use of the word like shows that she is directly sensing inside and that she is groping for words. This is usual when a client is finding words that exactly fit the felt sense. I notice the client's tears. Tears are often a sign that the client has touched upon a felt sense and that some release is happening.

T4: (Silence, 25 seconds) So you've already set the mind chatter out, and you're more with the sadness now.

I waited for 25 seconds to give her time to cry. I see that she has been able to set the mind chatter aside and that she can bring her attention to the sadness. I am using the word sadness now as a shorthand to refer to the larger felt sense with the tears in it.

C5: Yeah.

T5: So you could just be with that sadness in a friendly way and gently see what it's about.

I remind her to keep a friendly, gentle attitude toward her sadness, to give it a friendly hearing. Clients usually find this reminder helpful.

C6: (Silence, 20 seconds) Well, it feels like it wants to be acknowledged, first of all.

She is able to listen to her sadness and notice what it wants at the present moment.

T6: So first it wants to be acknowledged.

I could have reflected, "It feels like it wants to be acknowledged first of all" to reflect her tentative manner. But my more definite reflection doesn't keep her from further exploration. I reflect in a tentative manner in the sound of my voice.

C7: Because I stay so busy doing things, it feels like this is a part of me that just wants to be—not doing.

Some explicit meaning is now emerging from the feeling. She continues to use the word like. *This indicates that she is sensing into what is vague and new.*

T7: So this is a part of you that wants to be—not doing, rather than being busy all the time.

C8: Yeah. (Client cries quietly; silence, 10 seconds) (Client sighs; silence, 25 seconds) I think like this is a losing battle. So it's finally like it feels like it can express.

I interpret her sigh to mean that her attention is going even deeper into her body. She seems to be working as indicated by her attention going down into her torso area. So I remain quiet until more meaning emerges.

T8: So it's been feeling like it's in a losing battle, but now it feels like it can express.

I give a reflection, this time using her word like.

C9: That's the feeling I get right now.

T9: Umhm.

C10: (Silence, 15 seconds) Like it's so sad that it can't just *be* sometimes.

T10: Umhm. Like that part is really sad that you can't just *be* sometimes.

The client is at a deep level, and she is in process, so I reflect her words almost exactly.

C11: Yeah, that the doing side always seems to win.

T11: Umhm.

C12: Oh boy (tears). Oh boy. (Silence, 15 seconds) I don't know. (Client opens eyes and looks at me.)

The client looks overwhelmed by the sadness and seems to be wondering what to do next.

T12: I wondered if it would be helpful to set that whole thing out at a little distance to see both the doing side that always seems to win and the sad part that just wants to be sometimes and notice that whole thing.

Because the client seems stuck and confused in her process, I make a suggestion that she see and feel the whole issue (both sides of the conflict) at a little more distance.

C13: (Client closes eyes again.) O.K., so set that out so I can see both?

She is asking for clarification.

T13: Yeah, so you can see and feel both, and also so you can see beyond the edges of both of them.

I give her more explanation. The client needs to be able to see beyond her issue to realize that her life is greater than the issue. So I suggest that she see "beyond the edges of it" while still feeling it.

C14: (Silence, 20 seconds) Hmm. (Client smiles.) So, I get an image of like a fighting ring. (She laughs.)

The client's smile and laugh indicate a step of easing from having found more distance. Something new, a new image, emerges from having been able to tolerate the discomfort of holding both sides of the conflict.

T14: A fighting ring.

I give a reflection.

C15: Except they're not in the corners. They're on the sides, opposite sides. Especially when you said the borders.

The client continues to be able to observe the image and let it unfold.

T15: Ah, so the ropes are like the borders or the edges.

I give a reflection.

C16: Yeah.

The client indicates that I have understood her.

T16: And you can see everything connected to that whole issue, including everything—maybe what's connected from your childhood.

I frequently make a suggestion about noticing childhood connections when a client seems to be working on an issue regarding a long-term approach to life.

C17: Oh, what I see is like a spotlight coming down from above onto the stage. And so the part outside of it is dark, outside of the ring.

The client doesn't pick up on my suggestion to notice childhood connections. This is fine. It was only meant to be used if helpful to her process. The client continues her process on her own.

T17: Yeah.

C18: And it also feels like I don't know how to bring it together.

T18: Uh-huh.

C19: Yeah, like they had to stay on their separate sides.

T19: Umhm, (Silence, 5 seconds. The client is looking more tense.) And what's the worst of that whole thing for you? You might check that with your feeling.

The client seems to be a little stuck as indicated by more tension on her face and in her body. So I suggest an open-ended Focusing crux question. To answer the question, the client has to sense the whole problem. I point her back to her feeling or felt sense. If this were only an image without feeling, it would not be Focusing. An image in Focusing has feeling and meaning accompanying it.

C20: (Silence, 5 seconds) The worst seems to be that it feels like I have to *choose* all the time. I have to choose all the time, like I can't be while I'm doing, or like I'm always having to choose to do. Like it's not much of an option. (Client cries.)

The open-ended crux question has brought some new meaning and more feeling.

T20: Like it seems you always have to choose to do.

C21: Like I have no choice, really. Like I'm given a choice with no options.

T21: Umhm, a choice with no options. And how does that feel inside?

I reflect the client's words. Then I point her back to her felt sense with my question.

C22: (Silence, 8 seconds) Oh— like I feel—like my stomach feels like it's in knots. (Client cries.) And the part of me that wants to be feels—um—abandoned or not acknowledged (the client sounds surprised).

The client is paying attention to her bodily experiencing. More new, explicit meaning comes, as indicated by her surprise.

T22: So your stomach feels like it's in knots. The part that just wants to be feels abandoned or not acknowledged.

C23: Umhm. Yeah. (Client cries. Silence, 10 seconds)

T23: And there's still some sadness there too.

I notice that the client still looks sad.

C24: Yeah, I was thinking when I was a child, I did a lot of doing.

T24: So this is similar to when you were a child when you did a lot of doing.

C25: Well my parents basically wanted me to do this and do that and accomplish this and do well at that and I did (Client cries).

The client is probably not Focusing now, because she is talking in rapid, complete sentences. She is probably remembering and explaining the situation to me.

T25: So there were a lot of things your parents wanted you to do well at and you did that.

I continue to reflect to let her know I am with her and understand what she is saying.

C26: Umhm, and I felt that they wanted me to do that because they loved me and they wanted me to excel in school. And I enjoyed doing most of it anyway.

T26: Umhm, so you enjoyed doing most of it anyhow, and you could see they wanted you to do well because they loved you.

C27: Right. (Silence, 6 seconds)

T27: And how does this whole thing feel now?

When she pauses and seems to have completed her explanation, I point her back to her felt sense, to her implicit experiencing.

C28: It seems like I would like resolution of learning how to be able to choose or how to do both or how to feel peaceful at doing and not feel like I have to go, go, go—that I'm feeling the peace as I'm doing, the feeling of being able to feel centered in the midst of doing.

T28: So part of you would like resolution or to feel centered in the midst of doing. (Silence, 5 seconds) How does that whole thing feel in your body now?

I am not sure whether her answer came from her feeling or only her intellect. So I ask the felt sense question again.

C29: It feels calming. It also feels possible, which makes me feel hopeful.

The answer seems to have come from her feeling, as shown by the change in feeling. The feeling has now released into a calming and hopeful feeling.

T29: So it feels calming and possible and hopeful.

C30: Hmm. Feeling hopeful also makes me feel more joy, feeling more joy.

T30: So there's also feeling more joy there too.

C31: (Silence, 15 seconds) Hm.

T31: What came there?

When the client said, "Hm," she seemed to have discovered something new, so I ask about it.

C32: There's a part of me that goes, "How?" Like in the ring, I'm in the center. So I look this way, and I look that way, and say, "How? How do I get these two to-gether?" See, I'm in the middle.

More new, explicit meaning emerges.

T32: So the two figures are still on either side.

C33: Yeah, but they're not like real fighters looking to tear each other up. So they're willing to look at the pos-sibilities now.

T33: So, they're willing to look at the possibilities now. (Silence, 8 seconds) So maybe you could go inside and ask, "What does this whole thing need?" or "How would this whole thing feel if it were all O.K.?"

The client's nonverbal expression seems to indicate she is drifting away a little. So I tentatively suggest that she ask a felt shift question. Notice how I couch the question in a sug-gestion to make it easy for the client to reject the question if it is not helpful for her process. I offer two possible felt shift questions and let the client decide which of the two she would like to ask herself.

C34: (Silence, 5 seconds) If it were all O.K., it would feel integrated.

The client chooses to ask the second question and receives an answer.

T34: Can you get a feel of that in your body?

Again, I check if the answer came from her feeling and not her intel-lect only.

C35: (Silence, 7 seconds) The feeling I get is whole and integrated. You know, they're moving together within my body and flowing together as in a spiral or circle.

Again she confirms a feeling that goes with the meaning. She has started experiencing a felt shift.

T35: So it would feel whole and integrated and flowing together in a spiral or circle.

My reflection does not capture her meaning exactly because I was too tentative in that I added the word would.

C36: Within my body.

The client corrects me by restating a phrase from C35 that is important for me to say back.

T36: Within your body.

Whenever a client repeats words that have previously been said, I know that they are especially important for me to reflect. So I reflect her words exactly.

C37: So it's not like I have to choose. (Silence, 3 seconds) Hm.

T37: What came there?

Again, I ask about her "Hm," as in T31.

C38: A feeling of real peacefulness and serenity and flowing, a real smooth flowing movement, like I don't have to do any thing. I just go along with what's happening.

T38: So there's peacefulness and serenity and flowing, and you don't have to do anything. You just go along with what's happening.

C39: And then there's no need for a ring anymore.

T39: No need for a ring anymore. (Silence, 5 seconds) How does it feel now, this whole thing?

Here I am not so concerned that she check with her felt sense. I realize that she has experienced a felt shift. My question is simply a way of tracking her process.

C40: (Silence, 8 seconds) Peaceful. (The client looks very peaceful.)

T40: So now it feels peaceful. (Silence, 10 seconds) Would it feel right yet to ask how you experience God with this whole thing?

Here I ask a spiritually oriented Focusing question to help her stay with her felt shift and possibly amplify it. Notice how I embed the spiritually oriented question in another question, "Would it feel right yet to ask" I want to make it easy for her to reject the question if she has a need to do so. For example, she could easily say, "It doesn't feel right to ask that now."

C41: (Silence, 10 seconds) Hmm. I hear God saying, "Now this is how I'd like you to be."

T41: So you hear God saying, "Now this is how I'd like you to be."

C42: Like, "This is how it is to live in peace."

T42: Umhm, "This is how it is to live in peace."

C43: Like I have a feeling of opening up to greater joy, to—um—more possibilities—um—anything that is to come.

T43: So you have a feeling of opening up to greater joy, to more possibilities, anything that is to come. (Silence, 15 seconds) Is this a good stopping place?

Because the client has stayed with her felt shift for some time now, I ask if this is a good stopping place. Had she not spent much time with her felt shift, I might have said, "You can stay with that feeling as long as you like, and when you are ready to stop, you can let me know."

C44: Yeah. (Client slowly opens eyes.)

Comments

After the Focusing part of a session has been completed, I usually review places of easing to help a client reexperience and integrate these places. When I reviewed the session with this client, I said that she seemed to experience a step, or a degree of easing, when she received the image of a fighting ring (C14). She agreed and said that it was helpful to set the whole conflict between doing and not doing out at a little distance to see and feel the whole thing.

The client agreed with me that she had a more complete felt shift after I asked her the question, "How would this whole thing feel if it were all O.K.?" (T33). When I asked her if the "God question" was helpful, she said that it "opened up the feeling and helped it get bigger."

This example involves both spiritual content and process. The example has spiritual content in that it refers to God and because it refers to being in "flow." It has spiritual process because the client pays attention to vague bodily feelings and lets them unfold into clearer meanings. In the process she experiences bodily felt release with feelings such as peacefulness, serenity, and flowing. The client is able to accept and integrate a previously ignored part of herself, the part of her that wants only to be. In the process of integration, this part, along with the doing part, is transformed into a flowing spiral.

Conclusion

As seen in this excerpt, the Focusing Method has a simplicity, yet it is powerful. Much can happen in a short period of time. Certainly, Focusing is a tool for brief therapy.

This client could have spent the entire session telling me about her busy schedule and how she has difficulty taking time to relax or "just be." Instead, she experienced real change in 20 minutes of Focusing. How does this change happen? When a client pays attention to the implicit body sense as a whole, further steps come, and change occurs (Gendlin, 1996). For this reason, many clients who have learned Focusing insist that I spend a part of the counseling session guiding them in Focusing.

CHAPTER

How Counselors Can Explore
Their Own Spirituality

This chapter summarizes a number of counselor competencies for working with the spiritual dimension in counseling. A workshop for training counselors in these competencies is described, and exercises used to help counselors explore their own spirituality are presented. Directions for using the exercises are included.

The Association for Spiritual, Ethical and Religious Values in Counseling (ASERVIC), a division of the American Counseling Association, has endorsed a Summit on Spirituality to develop a list of professional counselor competencies regarding the spiritual dimension in counseling. It is highly recommended that these competencies be met by all mental health professionals working in clinical settings. Training in the spiritual dimension needs to be a part of every graduate counseling program. It is recommended that mental health professionals continue to explore their own spirituality in therapy, supervision, course work, and workshops.

Many of these competencies can be summarized by the following three general competencies: (a) The counselor can facilitate the psycho-spiritual growth process by helping clients work through religious and spiritual problems, enhance already existing spiritual experiences, and find new life-giving connections to spirituality; (b) the counselor can demonstrate openness to, empathy with, and acceptance of a variety of religious and spiritual content; and (c) the counselor can identify and describe his or her own beliefs regarding spirituality and actively engage in exploring those beliefs further.

Learning to use the Experiential Focusing Method to work with spiritual issues is a highly effective way of meeting all three competencies. Until now this book has shown how the Focusing Method can be used to meet the first two competencies. In this chapter I show how the Focusing Method can be used to help counselors identify and explore their own feelings and beliefs about spirituality. I show how this can be done through special Focusing exercises that are oriented toward exploring spirituality.

These exercises were developed to help counselors explore their spirituality in my workshop, Integrating Spirituality in Counseling. This workshop was first evaluated in a research project funded by ASERVIC. Participants who attended the workshop reported that it helped them feel more at ease and confident about approaching spirituality with their clients.

In the workshop I offer a definition of the spiritual experience, explain the Focusing method, and present guidelines for applying the Focusing method to psychospiritual issues in counseling. Participants experience the Focusing process and are then supervised in using the Focusing Method to help other participants with their psychospiritual concerns. Counselors are taught to use Focusing to process their own psycho-spiritual issues. If mental health professionals have difficulty following a client's experiencing process or have blocks to working with spiritual experiences in which clients use content different from their own, they may use the Focusing method to continue to process their feelings until they are prepared to work with a wide variety of clients.

Throughout the workshop counselors explore their own spirituality in a series of experiential exercises that are included in this chapter. In their evaluations of the workshops, many participants reported that this part of the workshop was most meaningful to them. Mental health professionals said that the exercises helped them integrate the theory presented in the workshop. They reported that the exercises helped make their faith more personally relevant and that the exercises helped them grow spiritually. The exercises from the workshop are included in this chapter so that they may be used by readers of this book for their own development.

How to Use the Exercises for Exploring Spirituality

When doing these exercises it is important to remember that Focusing tends to be easier if you have a listener, or at least someone with whom you can share your experience after completing an exercise. For this reason, you may want to find a friend or another mental health professional with whom you can practice.

If you choose to read these instructions to another person, avoid adding your own interpretations or comments during the exercises. The beginning preparation or relaxation part of the exercise may be adapted to the needs of the Focuser. For example, the Focuser may need a longer preparation time to become sufficiently relaxed.

When reading an exercise to another person, pause after each Focusing instruction and when pauses in parentheses are marked. Let the Focuser respond to the instruction before you continue with the next instruction.

If you are the Focuser and distressing feelings, such as pain or fear, arise during an exercise, it is important to Focus on these feelings. This can be done using the Focusing instructions in Appendix A. When Focusing, it is important to Focus on whatever is most present in a felt way.

After you have completed an exercise, you may wish to express what came to you in your process. For example, you may wish to express your process through writing, art, or movement. This often helps integrate new material received during the exercise.

Focusing on a Word or Phrase
That Has Spiritual Significance

In this exercise, participants in the workshop choose a word or phrase that has spiritual significance for them and Focus on it (Hinterkopf, 1990b, 1995b). Counselors reported that this exercise helped deepen their experience of their chosen word or phrase. Some people reported that words that they had previously said in a mechanical way become significant at an experiential level. For example, one counselor, a recovering alcoholic, said that the words "Let go and let God" had become automatic for him. After Focusing on these words, they again became meaningful to him because he could experience them in his body.

This exercise may be done with any sacred symbol, for example the yin yang of the Tao, the Jewish Tree of Life, the cross, or the crescent moon of Islam, to name just a few (Cave, 1993). These symbols cannot be understood from a rational, logical sequence perspective. However, they can be understood through Focusing, which involves a creative, nonlinear process that opens us to more than we can understand consciously. Some people call this the "mystery." Frequently these symbols, especially those used during one's childhood, are rich with meanings that may be explored numerous times.

Brunswick (1984) originally developed the idea of Focusing on a word or phrase that has spiritual significance for use with recitative prayer. This exercise can be done by reading any sacred text of your choosing (Hinterkopf, 1990b, 1995b). If you decide to Focus on a sacred text, read the text and recite the words to yourself slowly. You may wish to read the text a second time. While reading the text, notice which words you feel most strongly. These words can be your chosen words. Then continue with the exercise.

Instructions for Focusing on a Word or Phrase

Choose a word or phrase that has spiritual significance for you. Notice whether or not the word or phrase elicits a feeling in you. If the word or phrase does not stir up a feeling in you, you might try choosing a different word or phrase. (Pause)

Get comfortable and relaxed. Take time to be aware of your body. (Pause) Be aware of your arms and your hands, noticing your hands and what they're touching. (Pause) Notice your legs and feet, and what they're touching. (Pause) Let your awareness come into your body, your throat, your chest, and your abdomen. (Pause)

Now remember the word or phrase that you chose.

Repeat the word or phrase to yourself slowly. Notice the feelings the word or phrase stirs up in you.

As you keep repeating the word or phrase, find just the right words to describe your feeling.

Take time to be with your feeling. Notice whether you can feel a sense of "more" there. Gently keep your felt sense company for a while with an attitude of friendly curiosity.

As you notice your feeling, you can ask, "What is it about this word or phrase that leaves me feeling this way?" or "What is it about this word or phrase that is best or most meaningful for me?" Ask the question of your feeling and wait for an answer to come to you. When you get an answer, repeat it slowly and see if the feeling affirms the answer.

Then repeat the original word or phrase and notice what you feel. Describe your new feeling.

Focusing on Religious and Spiritual Art

In this exercise, participants choose a piece of art that has spiritual significance for them and Focus on the feelings that the art elicits in them. Counselors in my workshops frequently say that this exercise is their favorite. Most participants have not had the experience of Focusing on a piece of art. They reported having looked at art from a critical point of view or a historical point of view, but they had never thought of directly sensing it in their bodies. Participants found that the art or the part of the art that they chose had a deep connection to something in their lives. For example, it frequently pointed them to something important, something relatively new, or something that was needed in their lives.

I usually bring postcards from art museums with me to the workshop, so that each participant can choose their own piece of art. I have also led the exercise by having all the participants look at the same piece of art. After reading the Focusing instructions to the group, each person shares his or her experience. If the group has more than 10 or 12 people in it, I usually instruct people to form small groups to share their experiences.

Instructions for Focusing on Religious and Spiritual Art

Choose a piece of art that has spiritual significance for you and elicits feelings in you. Notice what it is about the art that draws your attention.

Get comfortable and relaxed and notice your breathing. (Pause) Gently let your awareness down into your body. (Pause)

Now you can remember what you saw in the piece of art that drew your attention.

Notice how the piece of art or a part of the art feels in your body. Take time to find just the right words to describe the feeling, resonating between the feeling and the words to describe the feeling.

Then you might ask yourself, "What in my life feels this way?"

Take time to notice how it feels in your body now.

You might also ask the feeling, "What's most important about this for me?"

Let the feel of the whole thing form in your body and find just the right words to describe it.

You might also ask your feeling, "What's best about this for me?"

Take time to be with your feeling and see what comes.

If you have an uncomfortable feeling, you might notice it, describe it, and promise to come back to it.

Take time to be with your feeling in a gentle, caring way.

When you are ready, you can bring your attention back into the room.

Focusing on Your Experience of God or a Larger Context

This exercise was developed to help people have a felt experience of the spiritual dimension (Hinterkopf, 1986, 1990b). I have been deeply moved while accompanying others through this powerful exercise.

Participants in my workshops who have experienced this exercise have said that it helped them reconnect with the God of their childhood, but now in an adult way. Others have said that the exercise helped them experience God with their bodies, rather than just with their heads. Still others have experienced God in a new, more constructive way, and others experienced nature and their larger context more fully.

In my workshops I usually use this exercise only when I have a small group of people, usually fewer than eight. During the exercise many positive and many uncomfortable feelings may arise in people. For this reason many people wish to Clear a Space before beginning the exercise. (Clearing a Space instructions can be found in Appendix A.)

Before giving the instructions, I explain that different people have different terms for referring to God. For example, Christians may choose to Focus on their relationship with Christ. Native Americans may wish to Focus on their experience of Mother

Earth. Muslims may wish to Focus on their sense of Allah. Others may find that they do not relate to the idea of a deity. They may wish to Focus on their experience of something greater than themselves or their experience of a larger background or context.

After giving the instructions for the exercise, I check with each person to determine whether any of the participants need help in further processing their feelings. After everyone has shared their experience, there is almost always a deep sense of group cohesion.

I wish to thank Ed McMahon and Peter Campbell for the term *caring, feeling presence,* which I use in this exercise.

Instructions for Focusing on Your Experience of God or a Larger Context

Get comfortable and relaxed. (Pause) Take time to notice your breathing. (Pause) Notice how the chair and the floor support your body. Then let your attention go down into your body, down into your throat, your chest, and your stomach area. Take time to create a caring, feeling presence for whatever comes. (Pause)

Then in a friendly, gentle way you can ask yourself, "What is my experience of God, my higher power, or something greater than myself right now?" or "How do I experience myself in a larger background or context right now?" Find the words for the spiritual dimension that best fit your experience.

Let the feeling of this whole thing form in your body and find just the right words to describe it. Take time to be with your feeling in a caring, gentle way, keeping an attitude of wondering curiosity.

You might ask your feeling, "What is it about my experience of God or something greater than myself that feels this way?" or "What is it about my experience in a larger background or context that feels this way?"

Then you can ask yourself, "How does this whole thing feel in my body now?"

You might ask your feeling, "What's best about this whole thing for me?"

If you have an uncomfortable feeling, you might notice it, describe it, and promise to come back to it. Welcome whatever comes.

Take time to be with your new feeling.

Focusing on the Gift You Need Today

In this exercise, participants are instructed to notice both their comfortable and uncomfortable feelings that they have toward life and then ask, "What gift is it that I need today?"

I often use this exercise on the second day of a workshop. Participants have said that this exercise helps them integrate what they have learned about spirituality into their daily lives.

This exercise includes Focusing on the predominant feeling one has toward life. Gendlin calls this a "background feeling." For example, people often feel somewhat afraid of life or somewhat angry at life, or they might find life burdensome and heavy. Frequently people have both a comfortable and an uncomfortable background feeling. Focusing on an uncomfortable background feeling tends to be a slow process but often leads to powerful changes in one's life.

Instructions for Focusing on the Gift You Need Today

Get comfortable and relaxed. (Pause) Pay attention to your breathing. (Pause) Notice how your body makes contact with the chair and how your feet make contact with the floor. (Pause)

As you let your awareness down into your body, get a feel for how your life is going these days. Take time to find just the right words to describe the predominant feeling or feelings you have toward life. You may find that you have both a comfortable and an uncomfortable feeling toward life. Welcome whatever comes.

Especially notice your uncomfortable feeling, and find just the right words or images to describe it.

Then take a few deep breaths and let your attention go to that place where there is a source of wisdom, power, and knowing. In that place you can ask, "What gift is it that I need today?"

As you receive the answer to the question, notice how your body feels as you imagine receiving the gift. Find just the right words or images to describe your new feeling.

If the answer brings constriction or dullness, ask the question again until it brings a sense of easing or more life energy.

Then you can ask the feeling, "What is it that's best about this for me?"

Notice your new feeling.

What Is Spirituality for Me?

I frequently use this exercise toward the end of a workshop to help participants get in touch with what is most important about spirituality for them.

Luke Lukens developed this exercise. Some of the wording for this exercise is my own.

Instructions for What Is Spirituality for Me?

Get comfortable and relaxed. (Pause) Notice your breathing. (Pause) To prepare for this exercise, you can let your attention come down into the center of your body, your throat, chest, and stomach.

Then you can ask, "What is spirituality for me?" Keep paying attention in your body until a vague feeling forms there, a feeling without words. You might feel the feeling in one part of your body or throughout your body. Find just the right words to describe the feeling.

From the feeling might come words or a phrase or an image that feels like an answer. Wait until something new stirs in you. You might ask the feeling, "What is it about spirituality that feels like this for me?"

Notice how spirituality feels in your body now. You might ask your feeling, "What's best about this for me?"

Take whatever time you need, and notice your new feeling.

Conclusion

The exercises in this chapter have been presented in the context of helping counselors explore their own spirituality. However, I have also used these exercises in other settings, such as medical and religious or spiritual settings. Workshop participants have frequently given me feedback that the exercises have helped them regain their sense of wholeness.

This book has presented an experiential approach to the spiritual dimension in counseling. The Experiential Focusing Method is far-reaching in its breadth and depth, and it may be used to help integrate and facilitate the spiritual experiences of all human beings. Because the skills described in this book may be used with any theoretical approach to counseling, counselors with different counseling approaches can use them to process their clients' spiritual and religious material.

Readers of this book are encouraged to continue study of the Focusing approach by reading the listed references. With this study and with direct training and supervision from Focusing teachers, counselors can gain the necessary expertise for applying this powerful method in their practice. I hope that the readers of this book will find the use of this method as life-changing in their own lives as in the lives of their clients.

Focusing Instructions

This Appendix contains a set of Focusing Instructions for one person to read to another. I recommend reading the following instructions to a friend or to another mental health professional and having them read these instructions to you.

Before attempting all of the Focusing Instructions, it is helpful to try several rounds of Clearing a Space. This helps break the more complex process into simpler steps, making it easier to learn. Clearing a Space, Step 1 of the Six Focusing Steps, includes many aspects of Steps 2, 3, and 4. For example, parts 1a and 1b of Clearing a Space includes Steps 2, 3, and 4 in the Focusing Steps. Part 2 of Clearing a Space involves finding a certain distance. After Clearing a Space, the Focuser can choose a problem and continue with Step 2 in the Focusing Instructions. On the other hand, the Focuser could instead decide to stop the process after Clearing a Space.

In the instructions, words in italics are not read aloud. They are included to help the person reading the instructions decide what to do next. Pause at the end of each numbered instruction and when pauses in parentheses are marked. Pauses are indicated for you to remain silent until the Focuser responds in a way that indicates that he or she has completed what the instruction called for. When the Focuser has completed the response, continue with the next instruction.

Throughout the process, notice whether the Focuser is keeping a friendly, or neutral, attitude toward whatever is present. If not, you might ask the Focuser, "I'm wondering if you are keeping a friendly, kind, patient attitude toward all of that?" If the Focuser seems overwhelmed by a problem and seems to need more distance, you might say, "I'm wondering if you need to step back from that problem and see the whole thing from a distance."

When the Focuser has difficulty identifying the feelings connected to a chosen problem, Clearing a Space may not be appropriate. After setting a problem (with the feelings) aside, the Focuser may not be able to get in touch with the feelings again. In this case, the Focuser may wish to choose a problem and start with Step 2 in the Focusing Instructions.

Focusing may seem simple, but it can be difficult to learn. I recommend learning Focusing with an experienced Focusing trainer whenever possible. Resources for this purpose can be found in Appendix B.

Preparation

Get comfortable and relaxed. (Pause)
Notice your breathing. (Pause)
Notice how your body makes contact with the chair and your feet with the floor. (Pause) Then you can let your awareness down into your body, down into your throat, your chest, and your stomach area. (Pause)

Step 1: Clearing a Space

1. Now you can ask yourself, "What's standing in the way of my feeling all O.K.?" (Pause) How does this whole thing feel in your body now?

If the Focuser has only an uncomfortable feeling, and not an issue, you can make the following suggestion:

You can ask yourself, "What in my life feels like this?"

If the Focuser has only an issue, and not an uncomfortable feeling, you can make the following suggestion:

You might try saying to yourself, "I feel perfectly okay about this whole thing," and notice the feeling that arises in you.

2. Then you can take the problem you have come up with along with the uncomfortable feelings about it, step back from it a little until you can see beyond the edges of it and notice the whole complexity involved there.

If the Focuser has difficulty setting the problem out, you might try making the following suggestion:

You could try seeing yourself with the problem at a distance, or you might ask your body what it needs to set the problem out.

3. Then you can set the problem aside, and you can ask yourself, "How would I feel if I didn't have this problem?" and notice your new feeling. (Pause) You can stay with that new feeling as long as you like, and when you are ready to continue, you can let me know.

Return to 1. Recycle 1, 2, and 3 with each issue until the Focuser has indicated that he or she has fully Cleared a Space. If the Focuser wishes, continue with Step 2.

Steps 2 through 6

If the Focuser wishes to begin the process with Step 2, a problem needs to be chosen and relaxation suggestions (found on the previous page) need to be given. Recycle Steps 2 through 5. The first time you reach Step 5, ask Question A, the second time Question B, and the third time Question C. (If the feeling changes, ask Question A again when you reach Step 5.) If a felt shift occurs at any time during the process, go to Step 6.

Then you can choose something to Focus on. (Pause)

Step 2: Getting a Felt Sense

How does that whole thing feel in your body now?

Step 3: Getting a Handle

Take time to be with your felt sense and notice the words or images that come to describe your feeling.

Step 4: Resonating

You can check if you have any other words to describe the feel of it. Where in your body do you feel that?

Step 5: Asking

Questions need to be given as suggestions, for example, "You might try asking yourself, 'What's the worst of this whole thing for me?'"
(a) What is it about this whole thing that leaves you feeling this way? (Return to Step 2.)
(b) What's the worst of this whole thing for you? (Return to Step 2.)
(c) What does this whole thing need? (Continue to Step 6.)

Step 6: Receiving

How does this whole thing feel in your body now?

If the Focuser has a good feeling when stopping the process, you can make the following suggestion:

Take whatever time you need to be with your new feeling. When you have completed your process, you can let me know.

If the Focuser has an uncomfortable feeling when stopping the process, you can make the following suggestion:

You can be with all of that in a caring way and promise it that you'll be back. When you are ready to stop, you can let me know.

APPENDIX

B

Resources for Learning Focusing

*E*lfie Hinterkopf is available to present workshops on the use of Focusing for spiritual issues, dream interpretation, creativity, and counseling. She is authorized to train students toward their Focusing trainer certification. If you are interested in sponsoring or organizing a workshop in your area or becoming a certified Focusing trainer, please contact:

> Elfie Hinterkopf, Ph.D.
> 8200 Neely Dr. #151
> Austin, Texas 78759
> Telephone: 512-343-1613
> E-mail: focus@texas.net
> Web site: http://lonestar.texas.net/~focus

For additional information about Focusing and for a teacher near you, contact the following organizations:

> The Focusing Institute
> 34 East Lane
> Spring Valley, New York 10977
> Telephone: 914-362-5222
> E-mail: info@focusing.org
> Web site: http://www.focusing.org

The Institute for Bio-Spiritual Research
P.O. Box 741137
Arvado, Colorado 80006
Telephone/Fax: 303-427-5311

References

American Psychiatric Association. (1994). *Diagnostic and statistical manual of mental disorders* (4th ed.). Washington, DC: Author.

Brunswick, L. K. (1984). A course on focusing and prayer. *The Focusing Connection, 1*(3). (Available from Focusing Resources, 2625 Alcatraz Ave. #202, Berkeley, CA 94705)

Campbell, P. (1996). Viewing therapy as a seamless whole. *The Focusing Connection, 13*(5).

Campbell, P., & McMahon, E. (1985). *Biospirituality: Focusing as a way to grow.* Chicago: Loyola University Press.

Cave, C. (1993). Focusing and sacred symbols. *The Focusing Connection, 10*(4).

Chandler, C. K., Holden, J. M., & Kolander, C. H. (1992). Counseling for spiritual wellness: Theory and practice. *Journal of Counseling and Development, 71*, 168–175.

Cornell, A. W. (1990). *The Focusing guide's manual.* Unpublished manuscript. (Available from Focusing Resources, 2625 Alcatraz Ave. #202, Berkeley, CA 94705)

Cornell, A. W. (1996). *The power of Focusing: A practical guide to emotional self-healing.* Oakland, CA: New Harbinger.

Cornell, A. W., & McGavin, B. (1996). "Standing it": The alchemy of mixed feelings. *The Focusing Connection, 13*(4).

Durak, G. M., Bernstein, R., & Gendlin, E. T. (1997). Effects of Focusing training on therapy process and outcome. *The Folio: A Journal for Focusing and Experiential Therapy, 15*(2), 7–14. (Available from The Focusing Institute, 34 East Lane, Spring Valley, NY 10977)

Frankl, V. E. (1984). *Man's search for meaning.* New York: Touchstone–Simon & Shuster. (Original work published 1946)

Friedman, N. (1995). *On Focusing: How to access your own and other peoples' direct experience.* Unpublished manuscript. (Available from Neil Friedman, 259 Massachusetts Ave., Arlington, MA 02174)

Gendlin, E. T. (1961). Experiencing: A variable in the process of thera-peutic change. *American Journal of Psychotherapy, 15,* 233–245.

Gendlin, E. T. (1962). *Experiencing and the creation of meaning.* New York: Macmillan.

Gendlin, E. T. (1964). A theory of personality change. In P. Worchel & D. Byrne (Eds.), *Personality change* (pp. 102–148). New York: Wiley.

Gendlin, E. T. (1966). Research in psychotherapy with schizophrenic patients and the nature of that 'illness.' *American Journal of Psycho-therapy, 20,* 4–16.

Gendlin, E. T. (1969). Focusing. *Psychotherapy: Theory, Research and Prac-tice, 6,* 4–15.

Gendlin, E. T. (1981). *Focusing.* New York: Bantam.

Gendlin, E. T. (1984). The client's client. In R. Levant & J. M. Shlien (Eds.), *Client-centered therapy and the person-centered approach.* New York: Praeger.

Gendlin, E. T. (1986). *Let your body interpret your dreams.* Wilmette, IL: Chiron.

Gendlin, E. T. (1996). *Focusing-oriented psychotherapy: A manual of the ex-periential method.* New York: Guilford.

Gendlin, E. T., Beebe, J., III, Cassens, J., Klein, M., & Oberlander, M. (1968). Focusing ability in psychotherapy, personality, and creativ-ity. In J. Shlein (Ed.), *Research in psychotherapy III* (pp. 217–241). Washington DC: American Psychological Association.

Gendlin, E. T., & Tomlinson, T. M. (1967). The process conception and its measurement. In C. R. Rogers, E. T. Gendlin, D. J. Kiesler, & C. B. Truax (Eds.), *The therapeutic relationship and its impact: A study of psychotherapy with schizophrenics* (pp. 109–131). Madison: University of Wisconsin Press.

Grof, S. (1976). *Realms of the human unconscious.* New York: Dutton.

Helminiak, D. (1987). *Spiritual development.* Chicago: Loyola University Press.

Hendricks, M. N. (1986). Experiencing level as a therapeutic variable. *Person-Centered Review, 1,* 141–162.

Hinterkopf, E. (1983). Experiential focusing: A three-stage training pro-gram. *Journal of Humanistic Psychology, 23,* 113–126.

Hinterkopf, E. (1984). An interview with Elfie Hinterkopf on "asking." *The Focusing Connection, 1*(3).

Hinterkopf, E. (1985a). How I teach people to identify the critic. *The Focusing Connection, 2*(1).

Hinterkopf, E. (1985b). Dealing with the critic. *The Focusing Connection, 2*(2).

Hinterkopf, E. (1986). Focusing on my relationship with God. *Kairos, 1*(2). (Available from Sheed & Ward, P. O. Box 419492, Kansas City, MO 64141)

Hinterkopf, E. (1988). What is spiritual in Focusing? *Kairos, 3*(1).

Hinterkopf, E. (1990a). Focusing questions to help integrate spiritual experiences. *The Focusing Connection, 7*(3).

Hinterkopf, E. (1990b). Focusing and spirituality in counseling. *The Folio: A Journal for Focusing and Experiential Therapy, 9*(3). (Available from The Focusing Institute, 34 East Lane, Spring Valley, NY 10977)

Hinterkopf, E. (1994). Integrating spiritual experiences in counseling. *Counseling and Values, 38*, 165–175.

Hinterkopf, E. (1995a, April). *Integrating spirituality in counseling.* Paper presented at the meeting of the American Counseling Association, Denver, CO.

Hinterkopf, E. (1995b). *Die Dimension Spiritualitat in Beratung und Therapie.* Unpublished manuscript. (Available from Focusing Zentrum Karlsruhe, Schillerstr. 89, 76352 Weingarten, Germany)

Hinterkopf, E., & Brunswick, L. K. (1975). Teaching therapeutic skills to mental patients. *Psychotherapy: Theory, Research and Practice, 12*, 8–12.

Hinterkopf, E., & Brunswick, L. K. (1981). Teaching mental patients to use client-centered and experiential therapeutic skills with each other. *Psychotherapy: Theory, Research and Practice, 18*, 394–402.

Hinterkopf, E., Brunswick, L. K., & Burbridge, R. (1975). Cultivating positive empathic self-responding. *Voices: The Art and Science of Psychotherapy, 11*(1).

Kelly, E. W. (1995). *Spirituality and religion in counseling and psychotherapy: Diversity in theory and practice.* Alexandria, VA: American Counseling Association.

Klein, M. H., Mathieu, P. I., Gendlin, E. T., & Kiesler, D. J. (1970). *The Experiencing Scale: A research and training manual.* Madison: University of Wisconsin Extension Bureau of Audiovisual Instruction.

Klein, M. H., Mathieu-Coughlan, P. I., & Kiesler, D. J. (1986). The Experiencing Scales. In L. S. Greenberg & W. M. Pinsof (Eds.), *The psychotherapeutic process: A research handbook* (pp. 21–71). New York: Guilford.

Leijssen, M. (1997). Focusing processes in client-centered experiential psychotherapy. *The Folio: A Journal for Focusing and Experiential Therapy, 15*(2), 1–6. (Available from The Focusing Institute, 34 East Lane, Spring Valley, NY 10977)

Lukens, L. (1992). Focusing: Another way to spirituality. *The Folio: A Journal for Focusing and Experiential Therapy, 10*, 65–72.

Mathieu-Coughlan, P. I., & Klein, M. H. (1984). Experiential psychotherapy: Key events in client-therapist interaction. In L. N. Rice & L. S. Greenberg (Eds.), *Patterns of change* (pp. 213–248). New York: Guilford.

McGuire, K. (1981). *Building supportive community: Mutual self-help through peer counseling.* Unpublished manuscript. (Available from Kathleen McGuire, 2344 Yorkwood Dr., Fayetteville, AR 72703)

Rogers, C. R., Gendlin, E. T., Kiesler, D. J., & Truax, C. B. (Eds.) (1967). *The therapeutic relationship and its impact: A study of psychotherapy with schizophrenics.* Madison: University of Wisconsin Press.

Shafranske, E. P., & Gorsuch, R. L. (1984). Factors associated with the perception of spirituality in psychotherapy. *Journal of Transpersonal Psychology, 16*, 231–241.

Shafranske, E. P., & Malony, H. N. (1990). Clinical psychologists' religious and spiritual orientations and their practice of psychotherapy. *Psychotherapy, 27,* 72–78.

Shea, J. (1987). *Religious experiencing: William James and Eugene Gendlin.* Lanham, MD: University Press of America.

Tomlinson, T. M., & Hart, J. T. (1962). A validation of the process scale. *Journal of Consulting Psychology, 26,* 74–78.

Walker, A., Rablen, R. A., & Rogers, C. R. (1960). Development of a scale to measure process change in psychotherapy. *Journal of Clinical Psychology, 16,* 79–85.

Young, D. C. (1994). Focusing and your victim. *The Focusing Connection, 11*(4).

Index

client to felt sense, 54-55
for felt sense, 20-21
   mother-daughter issue
     example, 22-23
in therapy session, 87

P

Panic attack case, 35-36
Past life experiences. *See also*
   Reincarnation
belief of client versus counselor and, 70
case example of, 70-71
Patient attitude, 26
Personal versus impersonal, 44
Phrase, with spiritual significance, 105-107
Positive feelings
in God experience Focusing,
   108, 109
in spiritual experiences, 71-73
Powerlessness, in face of inner
   critic, 46-47
Present versus past and future,
   44
Problems
certain distance and, 29-30
closeness to, 29-30
distance from, 30
feeling of, 29, 52
felt sense of. *See* Felt sense
intellectualization of, 29
internalization of, 37-38
inventory of, 52
itification of, 34
observer self and, 30
saying hello to, 33
setting aside, 52
spiritual, 3
too-close to, 34-37
visualization of, 34
Process. *See* Spiritual process
Process versus content, 10-11
Purpose, sense of, 7

Q

Question(s). *See also* Open-ended
   questions; Spiritually
     oriented questions
existential, 15
felt sense, 20-23
to felt sense, 63-64
felt shift, 66, 97
open-ended, 20-23, 54-55,
   61, 62, 87
versus closed-ended, 64
spiritually oriented, 80-82,
   83-84
statements versus, 64
what versus why, 64

R

Receiving, 55-56
example of, 56
instructions for, 116
Receptive attitude, 5
versus controlling attitude,
   25-26
Reflection
of felt sense words, 69
in therapy session, 87-88, 90,
   91, 92, 95
Reincarnation experiences,
   70-71, 79-80
Relaxation, before Focusing,
   51-52
Religious abuse, 74-75
Religious art, Focusing on,
   107-108
Religious experience(s)
negative, 74-75
positive, 74
Religious roots, exploration of,
   74-75
Religious tradition, learning
   about, 77-78
Religiousness, meaning of, 9

Spirituality. *See also* Counselors'
spirituality
  in cross-cultural counseling,
    12-13
  definition of, 11
  exploration of
    exercises for, 105
  Japanese concept of, 12-13
  meaning of, 9
  in nontheism, 10
  process definition of, 10-13,
    10-15
    example of, 14
    implications for practice,
      15-16
    process versus content in,
      10-11, 16
    transpersonal experiences
      in, 13
  Western concept of, 12, 13
Spiritually oriented questions
  closure of session and, 83
  confusing, 83-84
  content and, 80-81
  contraindications to
    in movement away from
      feeling, 82-83
    nonreligious persons, 84
    in tension or confusion, 83
  for felt shift, 81
  misuse of, 83
  with nonbeliever, 82
  with theistic person, 81
  in time of crisis, 82
Stillness, 5
Strength, personal, 7
Strengthening, versus inner
    critic, 46-47
Suggestion, as alternative to
    asking, 64
Suicide attempt, inner critic
    and, 43
Summit on Spirituality, 103
Symbols, religious, Focusing on,
    105-107

T

Theism
  in spiritual experience, 9-10
  terms in, 78-79
Therapy session, 87-101
  attitude in, 88, 90
  certain distance in, 88, 92
  open-ended questions in, 87
  pace in, 88
  review of, 100
  spiritually oriented question
    in, 89, 99
  steps in, 88
Thinking, before experiencing,
    84
Transcendent dimension,
    spiritually oriented
      questions for, 80-82
Transcendent growth process
  felt sense in, 12
  through Focusing steps,
    57–58
Transpersonal experiences, in
    spirituality, 13

U

Uncomfortable feelings
  in gift you need today exer-
    cise, 110
  in God experience Focusing,
    108, 109
  spiritual experience from,
    73-74

V

Verbal abuse, paternal, 46-47
Victims
  of inner critics, 42
  of verbal abuse, 47

Visualization
  for distancing, 34
  of inner critic, 47
  in setting aside, 52

W

Weight problem case, Focusing
    attitudes and, 27-28
Witness, 6

Word(s)
  client repetition of, 98
  for felt sense, 22-23, 54, 63
  nontheistic, 79
  reflection of versus para-
      phrasing, 87-88
  with spiritual significance,
      105-107
  theistic, 78-79